WHERE
HISTORY
HAPPENED

Peter Spearritt

WHERE HISTORY HAPPENED

The Hidden Past of Australia's Towns and Places

NLA PUBLISHING

CONTENTS

Indigenous and Torres Strait Islander communities should be aware that this book contains images and names of people who are now deceased.

all the fun of the fair!

SWAN HILL

The "Premier Town"
VICTORIA, AUSTRALIA

Swan Hill
centre of the Murray Valley . . . where past & present meet in the sunshine

Introduction

My fascination with Australian places comes from childhood road trips. Growing up in bayside Melbourne, surrounded by owner-builders, I saw frenzied activity on nearby houses every weekend. To escape the noise, we would have a day trip to Ringwood to visit a relative, a local GP who lived in an art deco mansion. Less salubrious, but even more atmospheric, was visiting Aunty Min, who lived in Newtown in Geelong, and rented rooms to Pakistani and Indian gentlemen studying textile production. Further afield, the lion dances, dragon procession and firecrackers of Chinese New Year in Bendigo proved both exciting and slightly scary.

When Queensland grandparents visited, we would venture as far as Wandiligong, and visit the goldfield sites—including Marong and Amherst—the places that both sides of the family had first set out for on landing by ship at Melbourne in the mid-1850s.

By car, we undertook an annual pilgrimage to visit grandparents in Brisbane and in Gympie over the Christmas school holidays. Like many Australians in the 1950s, we would camp by the side of the Princes Highway—much of it then unsealed—or in country town showgrounds. The showgrounds were usually run down, and so were most of the historic sites we visited, but to a child that gave them extra fascination. The Seahorse Inn at Boydtown on Twofold Bay in the mid-1950s was in absolute disrepair, as was the convict-built church that had lost its roof. Eden had its whaling museum, built in 1938, one of the few new structures in town. On one of these trips, we were stopped by gypsies in a horse-drawn caravan, who were keen to predict our future for a monetary consideration. In rural Australia, at that time, there were no 24-hour garages; indeed, if you didn't get petrol between 9am and 12 noon on Saturday in most country towns, you wouldn't be able to get any till after the weekend.

◄ Visitors to Swan Hill, which opened Australia's first 'folk and pioneer settlement' in 1966, could explore the *Gem* paddle steamer. Tourist brochures of this era rarely mentioned prior Indigenous occupation.

My maternal grandparents in Gympie had a capacious Queenslander, the reward for my grandfather's labour as a farmer and the owner of the local Ford dealership. This led to trips both to farms and nearby towns. Murgon sticks in my mind because it was the first time I saw Aboriginal children and adults in any number. Revisiting Murgon in the late 1970s, it was confronting to see that the local public toilets still had signs separating blacks from whites.

The rise of heritage consciousness in the 1970s and heritage legislation in all states over the next couple of decades, saw local councils, state governments and the federal government take a more active interest in our historical landscapes, hitherto the preserve of the National Trusts in each state and sometimes active local historical societies. Churches and municipal buildings were more likely to survive than historic houses or commercial buildings. Banks sold off at least half of their historic buildings in the 1980s and 1990s, preferring to lease commercial premises. Some bank headquarters survived in the capital cities, but were under threat in suburbs and country towns, especially those with floundering economies.

My professional engagement with the fate of heritage structures came in New South Wales in the 1970s and 1980s, writing assessments on a wide variety of buildings from the Ritz Cinema in Randwick, to the Balmain and White Bay power stations, and the Woolloomooloo Finger Wharf. A judge in an environmental tribunal, in contemplating the fate of the Ritz, said it was not the purpose of the heritage act to preserve 'the pale shadows of the great city interwar cinemas'. I found this extraordinary. Such a statement potentially meant that almost all suburban and country town cinemas could be demolished because they weren't as grand as the State Theatre in Market Street, Sydney, which mercifully survives.

Heritage assessments are supposed to take into account 'historical importance', which can be defined in many ways, from notable events that happened in a building, landscape or town, to engineering innovations and aesthetic importance. This last criterion truly is in the eye of the beholder.

▼ This tourist poster from the late 1960s played on the idea that few international visitors knew Australia offered 'historic ruins'.

Australia welcomes you

This is Australia? This is Australia! Historic ruins, Port Arthur, Tasmania. See them soon.

◄ The privately owned Australian National Airways, alongside the government-owned Trans Australia Airlines, enjoyed a two-airline agreement that kept air travel costs much higher than they are today.

▶ In the 1950s and 1960s, most families drove to their holiday destinations, so tips about how to fit everything in the car were welcome.

I have a particular penchant for abandoned industrial structures, but they are not everyone's cup of tea. When, with colleagues at heritage consultancy Godden Mackay Logan, I wrote an assessment of the importance of the redundant BHP steelworks plant in Newcastle, the *Newcastle Morning Herald* placed an image of the plant over Circular Quay, and quipped that if the Sydney Heritage Council (its real name is the New South Wales Heritage Council) wanted to preserve the plant, they could move it to Sydney.

Working with Marion Stell and John Young on the websites Queensland Places and Victorian Places—still the only two states to have such websites—made me appreciate even more the complex and intriguing histories of our places. I am indebted to friends and colleagues who have kindly commented on particular entries in this book, including Sheridan Burke, Jim Davidson, Alex Dellios, David Dunstan, Anne Gilmore, Stephen Foster, Susan Marsden, Christopher Power and John Rickard.

Where History Happened has stretched my own historical imagination and made me reassess many of these places. I have only written about places I have visited. A handful have strong personal connections, spanning the continent from Cooktown in North Queensland to New Norcia in Western Australia. Like all historians, I am dependent on a wide variety of local sources, especially informative local histories. Increasingly, the pertinent stories and often the evidence are to be sourced from websites, sometimes reliable, often quite misleading. The National Library's Trove website is a great boon to historians, enabling a search of hundreds of digitised newspapers. A book like this will not be free from error, and some of the grimmer events presented here will be debated for decades to come.

Where History Happened is written with the conviction that we should continue to explore our places and spaces, and attempt to understand the forces that have shaped them over time. There is no better place to start to understand a building, a township, a mine or a tramway than by exploration. If your appetite is whetted for greater understanding, the local historical society or local municipal library is a great way to start. With the ongoing boom in family history, more and more accounts are now finding their way into print and/or online. You will have your own views of where history happened, because of course it happened everywhere. We don't have places without histories, and there are umpteen places one could choose. In my selection here, I have only alighted on places that the public can explore. It is easy to wander around cities and towns and to enter public buildings, from railway stations and courthouses to post offices—though some of our capital city GPOs have recently been onsold to corporate interests and none of our state Government Houses are open to the public on a regular basis. In stark contrast, you don't need an invitation to explore most of our churches during the usual opening hours, and you are welcome to explore the monastic town of New Norcia at your leisure. You can go on a guided tour of some of our historic jails, and explore most of our important convict sites. You can't visit what remains of the BHP plant at Newcastle, but you can get some idea of twentieth-century industrial activity by visiting Cockatoo Island or the Ipswich Railway Workshops.

In the last two decades, both the federal government and state governments have displayed much less interest in actively preserving our heritage places, other than the most outstanding sites, from Port Arthur to Kakadu National Park. Much of our country town heritage is in a state of disrepair, with only the state National Trusts and local historical societies to barrack for it. In the cities, commercial values increasingly drive town planning and heritage decisions. Facades are often saved, but the history of the sites is lost. I hope that *Where History Happened* helps to rekindle public interest in historic preservation. Our many histories will always be the subject of debate, but it will be a richer debate if the places themselves are allowed to retain some sense of their history.

CANBERRA   *Federal Capital & Garden City*

AUSTRALIA

Australian Capital Territory

Making the Capital 'National'

In just over 100 years, Canberra—a purpose-built national capital—has become the nation's seventh largest city. To the visitor it offers all one would expect from a national capital, housing the federal parliament, the headquarters of most government departments and a wide array of cultural institutions, all open to the public. Most embassies are within a few kilometres of Parliament House, while Lake Burley Griffin offers walking and cycling trails. Beyond the lake, Canberra has developed car-based suburbs, serviced by freeways and a road system replete with roundabouts that bamboozle many visitors. The ski fields of the Australian Alps and the pristine beaches of the New South Wales south coast are each just a couple of hours drive away.

As a fledgling national capital, it took Canberra a long time to establish its centrality to Australian life. Not until 1927, when the federal parliament moved from Melbourne to Canberra's 'provisional' Parliament House ❶ did the capital have much to boast. In 1938, a promotional booklet reported a population of 8,000 plus two million trees and shrubs. The opening of the Australian War Memorial ❷ in 1941 gave Canberra its second commanding building. Though not as grandiose as Melbourne's Shrine of Remembrance nor as elegant as Sydney's Anzac Memorial in Hyde Park, the Australian War Memorial already had substantial museum collections, which the others did not. Offering an uninterrupted vista down Anzac Parade to Parliament House, the Memorial stood out in a brown landscape of empty paddocks, the promised lake still more than two decades away.

Canberra's inland location, partly for defence reasons, meant it could not be the first port of call for visitors by ship. The acquisition of Jervis Bay on the coast south of Sydney gave the Australian Capital Territory a port for naval purposes, but was hardly sufficient to welcome visiting dignitaries, let alone royalty. So when Queen Elizabeth II, the first reigning monarch to visit Australia, arrived from New Zealand on the SS *Gothic* in February 1954, she made landfall in Sydney, which is where she started her 'Royal Progress'. Over two-thirds of all Australians saw her during this two-month trip, not least because, as the historian Ken Inglis put it, finally Australians could see 'the face on the money, smiling in their own streets'.

After Prime Minister Menzies welcomed them in Sydney, the Queen and the Duke of Edinburgh flew into the Royal Australian Air Force base at Canberra Airport, as guests of the Governor-General, British war hero and field marshal Sir William Slim. The royal couple stayed at the Governor-General's residence in Yarralumla ❸, a doubled-gabled, three-storey house built in 1891 by a sheep grazier, which was the nearest thing Canberra had to a stately home.

◄ The twin lanes of Commonwealth Avenue Bridge over Lake Burley Griffin in 2012, with Parliament House ❹ in the background.

The Canberra Times proudly boasted that 'Canberra has sprung from village to world Capital'. The Queen presided over a joint sitting of parliament, but more remarkably unveiled the Australian-American Memorial **5**, commemorating the contribution of the United States to the war against the Japanese in the Pacific. British officials in Australia had opposed the Queen's unveiling of the memorial as it served to emphasise that, since the fall of Singapore, Australia could no longer rely on Britain for protection.

The United States had already opened the first purpose-built embassy **6** in Canberra in 1943, almost opposite the Prime Minister's Lodge. Its Georgian architecture mimicked colonial Williamsburg in Virginia. The British, with limited finances after the war, didn't get around to building their embassy until 1952, a modest, modernist structure, with a prominent site on Commonwealth Avenue.

When wartime Labor prime minister John Curtin managed to wrest control of citizens' income tax from the state governments, Canberra finally got its hands on the purse strings of the nation, but war debt and postwar reconstruction left little money for the national capital. The new Australian National University, established in 1946, had a great site near the city centre, Black Mountain and the projected lake, but substantial buildings did not appear for some years **7**. Liberal prime minister Robert Menzies became convinced that Canberra needed a real boost to live up to its claim to be the national capital. More public service departments began to move from Melbourne to Canberra, and the generously funded National Capital Development Commission, founded in 1957, selected locations for the Reserve Bank and the Mint **8**, with cultural institutions the next cabs off the rank, allocated prime lakeside sites. The opening of the neo-classical National Library **9** in 1968, designed by Walter Bunning, meant that Canberra could finally lay claim to the nation's largest library, a cultural centrality later reinforced with the opening of the High Court **10** and the National Gallery **11** further along the lake.

When Lyndon Baines Johnson became the first US president to visit Canberra in 1966, he saw a small but established city, alongside a lake lately filled with water, and reminiscent perhaps of Washington DC. He flew into Canberra where his bullet-proof Lincoln Continental car awaited him. Also there to greet him were anti-Vietnam protesters and pro-US wellwishers. Because of his retinue, LBJ didn't stay in Government House at Yarralumla—which after all houses the representative of the British monarch—instead taking over a couple of floors of the Rex, then Canberra's only luxury hotel. According to *The Canberra Times*, after getting drunk at a dinner hosted by Prime Minister Holt in the Lodge, the President had to be smuggled into the hotel via a back door. Built in 1959, the Rex still stands, much-renovated, on Northbourne Avenue **12**.

As Canberra gained momentum, nations vied for sites within cooee of the Parliamentary Triangle. The aftermath of the Second World War saw the Soviet

THE QUEEN IN FOUR CAPITALS

HER MAJESTY in a spectacular Canberra ceremony unveils the Australian National Memorial to America. The monument is a 258ft. high aluminium shaft, surmounted by an eagle of aluminium with outstretched wings.

▲ President Johnson ('LBJ') farewelling the Canberra crowd in 1966, while Prime Minister Harold Holt takes pride of place on the steps.

embassy representing a raft of 'socialist republics', while wartime enemies Germany and Japan established embassies in the mid-1950s. Dozens followed, from Europe, Africa, South America and especially Asia, where newly independent nations, including India, Pakistan, Indonesia and Malaysia, were keen to establish a presence 🚱 🚲. China, with the world's largest population, was noticeably absent.

One of the Whitlam Labor government's first acts was to give diplomatic recognition to China in December 1972. The following year, the Chinese government asked for advice about a location for a new embassy building, and the Department of Foreign Affairs suggested they contact local real estate agents. The Chinese government bought a large site just behind the British High Commission and home to the Commodore Motel, but construction of a new building did not start for another 15 years. The embassy 🚳, in Forbidden City style, opened in August 1990, a little over a year after the Tiananmen Square massacre in Beijing. Prime Minister Hawke had offered Chinese students in Australia asylum, and this was also claimed by some embassy employees. In 1995, the Australian Broadcasting Corporation reported that the embassy had been bugged during construction, with signals sent on to the United States Embassy via the nearby British High Commission. The Chinese Embassy almost doubled its building size in 2011, making it by far the largest embassy in Canberra. By that time, China was this nation's largest trading partner for both imports and exports.

Canberra today appears as a settled capital landscape. Most visitors from Sydney come by car, as it is only a three-hour trip, while other visitors fly in, as do almost all politicians and most senior bureaucrats. The city now boasts a spacious airport, but when parliament isn't sitting it can be quiet indeed. Sydney and Melbourne still dominate the nation's economy, as they did at federation. But Canberra rules the roost in diplomacy and foreign affairs, and 40 per cent of Commonwealth public servants reside there. While the city now has long tongues of suburban development, linked by an elaborate freeway system, its central landscapes of culture, education, diplomacy and government remain readily visible and accessible to the visitor, especially if walking or cycling around Lake Burley Griffin.

NOTE: All of Canberra's cultural institutions, along with the High Court, are open to the public. Government House, like its equivalents in each state capital, along with The Lodge, is open only occasionally, even though all are funded by the taxpayer. Small sections of embassies are open to the public for general enquiries, although visa applications are often handled by a separate office. Entry to most major public service buildings is often now restricted to people who have a prior appointment with a public servant.

Explore the history

1. **OLD PARLIAMENT HOUSE**
King George Tce, Parkes

2. **AUSTRALIAN WAR MEMORIAL**
Treloar Cres, Campbell

3. **GOVERNMENT HOUSE**
Dunrossil Dr, Yarralumla

4. **PARLIAMENT HOUSE**
Parliament Dr, Barton

5. **AUSTRALIAN–AMERICAN MEMORIAL**
Field Marshal Sir Thomas Blamey Sq, Russell

6. **EMBASSY OF THE UNITED STATES OF AMERICA**
Moonah Pl, Yarralumla

7. **AUSTRALIAN NATIONAL UNIVERSITY**
Acton

8. **ROYAL AUSTRALIAN MINT**
Denison St, Deakin

9. **NATIONAL LIBRARY OF AUSTRALIA**
Parkes Pl, Parkes

10. **HIGH COURT OF AUSTRALIA**
Parkes Pl, Parkes

11. **NATIONAL GALLERY OF AUSTRALIA**
Parkes Pl East, Parkes

12. **REX HOTEL**
150 Northbourne Ave, Braddon

13. **INDIAN HIGH COMMISSION**
3–5 Moonah Pl, Yarralumla

14. **HIGH COMMISSION OF PAPUA NEW GUINEA**
39–41 Forster Cres, Yarralumla

15. **EMBASSY OF THE PEOPLE'S REPUBLIC OF CHINA**
Coronation Dr, Yarralumla

◄ Parliament House, with the modest Old Parliament House in front of it, both aligned to Mount Ainslie, and overlooking the Australian War Memorial.

Old Parliament House

The scene of 61 years of political argy-bargy, grand gestures and grandstanding, Old Parliament House is one of the most atmospheric places to visit in the nation's capital. On soft leather pews in its Senate and House of Representatives chambers—which visitors can sit on today—Paul Keating identified 'boxheads', 'scumbags' and 'mangy maggots' among his political opponents and the nation's leaders debated sending young men to fight and die in Vietnam. On its front steps in November 1975, dismissed PM Gough Whitlam imperiously intoned to a thronging crowd that 'nothing will save the Governor-General'. On the same steps in 1927, Wiradjuri Elder Jimmy Clements stood barefoot at the building's grand opening, looking out at what is now the site of the Aboriginal Tent Embassy, in a powerful display of Aboriginal protest and the politics of visibility.

Arriving in Canberra by car or aeroplane, newcomers could be forgiven for mistaking the elegant white building just up the rise from the High Court and the National Library as the nation's Parliament House, before sighting the 1988 version built into the top of a hill, partially covered by lawns and surmounted by a huge flagpole.

Like many Australians, the first time I saw Parliament House in Canberra was on a school excursion. Very few people got to Canberra before the 1950s. It had a tiny population, and took at least seven hours on rough and windy roads to drive to from Sydney and 16 hours from Melbourne. Most visitors, including parliamentarians, came by train, and from Melbourne that meant getting off at Yass Junction and catching a bus to the national capital. The majority of Australians had only seen their federal parliament on black and white Movietone newsreels and in newspaper photographs.

It took some time for the nation to take Canberra seriously. The federal constitution had specified that the purpose-built national capital be within New South Wales, but at least 100 miles from Sydney, an attempt to ensure that the colonies of New South Wales and Victoria would support the federation referendum. The federal government had to buy sheep stations for the site of Canberra, and acquire land on the coast at Jervis Bay, because no-one had ever envisaged a capital that didn't have a port.

The question of where to house the new parliament in the interim was solved by taking over the Victorian Parliament House—a Roman Revival edifice, built in 1856 and funded by gold revenue. The New South Wales Parliament House, a hotchpotch of buildings incorporating the old rum hospital, simply wasn't up to the task. Federal parliament remained sitting in Melbourne until 1927 and most government departments remained headquartered there until the 1950s.

◀ Parliament House, photographed by Frank Hurley in 1938, at which time it was the largest building in a still tiny federal capital.

◄ Wiradjuri Elder Jimmy Clements sits in the dust outside Parliament House in 1927. He had walked barefoot from the Riverina to attend the opening.

The location of the new Parliament House was one of the key tasks facing the 137 entries submitted for the design of the new federal capital. The winning entry, by Walter Burley and Marion Mahony Griffin of Chicago, announced in 1912, placed the House roughly where it ended up, with an ornamental lake as its primary vista. The lake itself, created by diverting the Molonglo River, didn't take in water until 1963.

The 'provisional parliament house', designed by John Smith Murdoch, had sombre chambers for the House of Representatives, with green seating, and the Senate, with red seating, based on the colour scheme of the British Houses of Parliament. The public could readily mix with their parliamentarians in King's Hall. But out the back, as a cost saving measure, some of the exterior walls were made of fibro.

Having secured the Duke (later King George VI) and Duchess of York to open the new structure, the powers that be assumed that thousands would turn up to mark the historic occasion, with Dame Nellie Melba singing the national anthem, *God Save the King*. Canberra only had a population of 6,000 and attendance at the event proved sparse, so 10,000 uneaten meat pies had to be buried at the Queanbeyan tip. Canberra also had the drawback of being, until 1928, without liquor, so if you wanted a beer to celebrate you were better off in the nearby New South Wales town of Queanbeyan; at least it had some pubs.

▼ A helicopter view of Canberra at dawn, ringed by mountains and hot air balloons. Parliament House is in the foreground, with the Civic Centre in the middle ground and the Black Mountain Telecommunications Tower to the left.

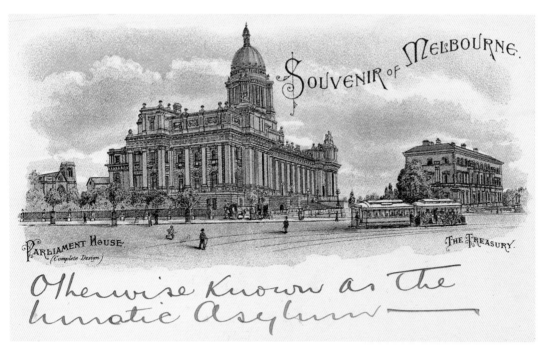

SOUVENIR OF MELBOURNE.

PARLIAMENT HOUSE.
(Complete Design)

THE TREASURY.

Otherwise known as the lunatic Asylum —

▲ Melbourne had a much grander Parliament House than Sydney, so it became the home of the new Commonwealth Government until 1927. The cupola depicted in this 1903 image was never built.

▶ Sheep were still allowed to graze in front of Parliament House in the 1940s. Canberra is situated on land once home to the Ngunnawal people, appropriated by Europeans for a sheep station.

▲ Dame Nellie Melba
sings *God Save the
King* at the opening of
Parliament House in
1927, with Prime
Minister Stanley
Melbourne Bruce and
Mrs Bruce standing at
the top of the stairs.

▶ Labor Prime Minister
Gough Whitlam on the
same stairs 48 years
later, speaking to the
media after he
had been sacked by the
Queen's representative
in Australia, the
Governor General Sir
John Kerr.

With the coming of television, you could see federal politicians being interviewed on the front steps of Parliament House from your lounge room. The most viewed and most memorable of these events was when Governor General Sir John Kerr's secretary, David Smith, read out the pronouncement sacking the Whitlam Labor government in November 1975. A towering Whitlam quipped in response, 'well may we say 'God save the Queen', because nothing will save the Governor General'.

Old Parliament House is now open to the public as the Museum of Australian Democracy. It retains an intimate atmosphere, unlike its replacement up the hill, where the politicians now have their own entry points into a carefully crafted but gargantuan building, which boasts 4,700 rooms. Today, most of us see our politicians being waylaid for doorstop interviews as they sidle in or out of the new Parliament House, on the evening news or on the web.

A visit to Old Parliament House is a return to a smaller, more intimate Australia, where oratory, quips and radio broadcasts were the order of the day. The 'House' retains its old world charm, while the exhibitions traverse a century of national political history.

▲ Old Parliament House retains its original charm. The Aboriginal Tent Embassy—seen here in tents and banners at right— has been removed and then re-established a number of times since its creation in 1972.

DELIGHTFUL VIEWS FROM
THE CARRIAGE WINDOWS

New South Wales

Broken Hill

Broken Hill sits in a desert-like landscape. Its rich industrial history can be seen in a remarkable number of structures, from the remnants of its vast mines to the banks and hotels of a once very wealthy city. It is best viewed from the recently built Miners Memorial, atop an artificial hill made of mine tailings. From here, you see the grand layout of the town, with its wide streets and scores of heritage-listed buildings. Mine workers here won a 35-hour week in 1920, the first workers in Australia to do so. But the mines were dangerous places, with many deaths. Broken Hill is also home to one of the oldest mosques in Australia and the Palace Hotel, known to cinema-goers around the world from the scene where three Sydney drag queens win the respect of the locals in *The Adventures of Priscilla, Queen of the Desert*.

Broken Hill is a name familiar to most Australians, even if they have never visited it. It shares, along with Qantas, the best known company name in Australia, Broken Hill Proprietary Limited, BHP for short ❶ ❷. The explorer Charles Sturt referred to a 'broken hill' in his diary in 1845. The Wiljakali people occupied the area and faced less immediate settler aggression than tribal groups who lived on the rivers, including the Darling. While some retained their traditional mode of living for decades, men were often employed as shearers or cattlemen and women as domestic help.

When the writer George Farwell came to Broken Hill with artist Roy Dalgarno to produce their elegant book *Down Argent Street: The Story of Broken Hill* (1948), they likened the town to something you might find in the American west.

The personality of the great mines is worked into the fabric of the city everywhere. Their great shaftheads and surface plants dominate the scene, posted like sentinels at either end of The Hill, or what has been left of it … As you drive out to a suburb the buildings abruptly fall away, leaving only a mountainous foreground of tailing dumps, white or copper hued in sunlight, and dun brown masses of slimes—man-made hills that long ago became permanent features of the landscape.

Farwell wrote of a city that never appeared to sleep, with miners on shift work and ore trains leaving at all hours to the smelters at Port Pirie on Spencer Gulf.

The discovery of gold in the 1850s put Australia on the world's mining map. People came from America, Europe and China to seek their fortunes. In 1883, when the boundary rider Charles Rasp formed a small syndicate to mine a great ironstone outcrop in the far west of New South Wales, they thought they would find tin.

◀ This photograph, taken in 2016, conveys a sense of both isolation and civilisation. Government buildings, hotels, churches and schools dominate the townscape, while the railway and the tailings remind us of a long history of mining.

Instead, they ended up having leases over some of the world's richest silver, lead and zinc deposits near Broken Hill ③. Unlike gold, these metals were not simply there for the taking. BHP, formed in 1885, faced technical and logistical challenges in mining and processing ore bodies.

Broken Hill grew very quickly. A population of 17,000 in 1889 had more than doubled to 35,000 in 1914, putting Broken Hill on the map as the then third largest city in New South Wales. They came from many parts of the world. In today's terms, it could be described as Australia's most multicultural city of the time. The diverse population was not immune to events on the other side of the globe. On 1 January 1915, by which time Britain and other European imperialist powers had declared war on the predominantly Muslim Ottoman Empire, two former cameleers—one an ice cream vendor, the other a local imam and halal butcher—opened fire on a picnic train, killing four people before they themselves were shot by police.

▼ The BHP mine in 1892, where grit, poppet heads and chimneys dominate the landscape.

Both men hailed not from Turkey, as popular rumour had it, but from a region in what today is Pakistan, then under British rule.

Trade unions quickly formed around the mine and extraction processing industries. The Trades Hall ❹, built between 1891 and 1905, became the first building in Australia owned by unions, who also purchased the local newspaper *The Barrier Times* in 1908. This strong union tradition permeated all aspects of life in Broken Hill. In 1912, the bandsmen of Broken Hill, with the support of fellow citizens, raised funds to erect a fine memorial to the bandsmen of the *Titanic*, who bravely played on while the ship sank ❺. Broken Hill unionists won a 35-hour week in 1920, the first to do so in Australia. On my first visit, in 1988, an early morning walk led me to the Social Democratic Club ❻, whose name reflects the town's long history of active trade unionism. I had travelled from Parkes to Broken Hill on the *Silver City Comet*, the first air-conditioned train in the British Empire, which plied the rail line from Sydney from 1937 to 1989. On entering the Social Democratic Club just after 6am, one of the breakfast staff apologised for the fact that they were not allowed to serve beer until 7am.

At 22 hours to Sydney by train and only ten to Adelaide, most residents took their holidays in the South Australian capital. The architecture of Broken Hill, especially in the stone public buildings and many hotels, is often reminiscent of Adelaide. Today, visitors to Broken Hill arrive by air, usually from Sydney or Adelaide; by car (especially the grey nomads); or by train, the station being in a commanding position at the top of the town. They find a city of large public buildings ❼ ❽,

▲ The Barrier Social Democratic Club remains proud of its trade union origins, including battles over pay, working hours and safety.

◀ Frank Hurley's aerial photograph from the early 1960s shows hundreds of workers' cottages in a neatly subdivided, flat landscape. Most houses had tin roofs and some even had tin walls. Better-off households could afford electric fans, but most people sweltered in summer.

▶ The Afghan mosque is still a place of worship today, and has changed little since this photograph was taken in 1977.

substantial clubs and hotels **9**, and thousands of often very modest houses, many simply with tin roofs and tin walls. The streets peter out into the mulga desert after a few blocks. The city is full of surprises, including a mosque **10**, founded by Afghan cameleers in the early 1890s, and a synagogue **11** built in 1910. The cameleers flourished in the later decades of the nineteenth century, transporting wool as well as construction materials for the Overland Telegraph Line from Darwin to Port Augusta. Completed in 1872, this was the first coast-to-coast telegraphic landline in Australia. The Jewish population mainly came from Eastern Europe. While the synagogue closed in 1962, the mosque is still used as a place of worship. Both are overseen by the Broken Hill Historical Society and can be visited by the public.

With a rainfall of just 235 millimetres per year, the climate in this region of New South Wales is dry and dusty, unrelentingly hot in summer, cooling down overnight, with brisk cool winters. For some decades now, most houses have had evaporative air coolers on their roofs. Successive generations of miners and industrial workers, most arriving on the train from Adelaide, must have been shocked to see such a large town surrounded by what they regarded as a desert.

BHP ceased operations in Broken Hill in the late 1930s, by which time other mining companies had formed. BHP left behind an open-cut mine that George Farwell described in 1948 as:

forlorn as a dead planet. It has the air of a crater on the moon … Massive boulders and abandoned machinery sprawl down its flanks as though flung down the sheer sides of a mountain gorge. Upon the crest old iron lies everywhere

Such a large and isolated city produced an array of talented individuals, one of whom is actually named in honour of the city of her birth. After June Gough, a talented soprano from the Hill, won the *Sun* Aria singing competition, one of her teachers, Madame Mathy, suggested she replace the surname Gough with 'Bronhill', and under that name she travelled to London, her fare raised by local subscription.

▼ This photograph shows the synagogue some decades after it closed in 1962.

▶ Pro Hart's landscapes established him as a quintessential interpreter of Australian country town life.

▼ The photographer Wolfgang Sievers captures both the danger and the eerie majesty of miners at work in the North Broken Hill Mine in 1980.

In a long and successful career, she sang at Sadler's Wells, Covent Garden and later with the Australian Opera, her repertoire including both opera and musicals. Broken Hill also produced the actor Chips Rafferty **12**, famous for his portrayal of the laconic Australian male, and the artist Pro Hart, whose semi-naive paintings of inland Australian life, especially in mining towns, captured the imagination of many who grew up in the 1950s and 1960s. Living most of his life in Broken Hill, Pro Hart was usually to be found at his own gallery **13**, which remains, since his death in 2006, a popular attraction on the tourist circuit.

Eighty-eight per cent of Broken Hill's population of 18,500 is now Australian-born, and eight per cent is Indigenous. The city continues to decline slowly, although tourism has become an important part of the local economy, along with mining, health and education. Waves of tourists fly in, drive in or come off the *Indian Pacific* train. Most visit the Palace Hotel's foyer **14** made famous by the movie *The Adventures of Priscilla, Queen of the Desert*, try out a pub or two and make the pilgrimage to the Line of Lode Miners Memorial, the striking architectural feature at the apex of a manmade mini-mountain of tailings **15**. Deliberately fashioned in rusting iron, the memorial lists the names of more than 800 miners who died in mine accidents over the last 140 years. From here, one gets a magnificent view of the city, its close-knit suburbs, and the desert beyond. Many people—including both the workers and the bosses—made money here, but not all lived to tell their tales.

Explore the history

1 SYNDICATE OF SEVEN SCULPTURES
Sulphide St

2 BHP CHIMNEY
McGillivray Dr

3 KINTORE RESERVE
Blende St

4 TRADES HALL
Cnr Blende and Sulphide Sts

5 THE TITANIC MEMORIAL
Sturt Park

6 BARRIER SOCIAL DEMOCRATIC CLUB
218 Argent St

7 POST OFFICE
260 Argent St

8 FORMER ST JOSEPH'S CONVENT
Sulphide St

9 ROYAL EXCHANGE HOTEL
320 Argent St

10 MOSQUE
Cnr William and Buck Sts

11 FORMER SYNAGOGUE
165 Wolfram St

12 BILLYGOAT HILL PLAQUES
Argent St

13 PRO HART'S GALLERY
108 Wyman St

14 PALACE HOTEL
227 Argent St

15 MINERS MEMORIAL
Federation Way

Byron Bay

Byron Bay has a surprising history. In just 60 years it has gone from being a dirty, industrial town to one of the nation's most popular beach destinations. The stench from the piggery, the abattoir and the whaling station—with whale carcasses cut up just off the main street—has been replaced with throngs of Australian and international holiday-makers. The township has lost much of its intimacy to modern tourism, but the camping grounds retain a modest charm, and the surf beaches remain unspoilt. Looking north towards Brunswick Heads from the famous lighthouse, you can't see a structure over three stories. When you look at the Gold Coast from Point Danger, on the New South Wales–Queensland border, just 70 kilometres north, you are confronted with a coastline dominated by scores of high-rise apartments.

I f you take a walk along the continent's most easterly beaches at dusk, you see the comforting regularity of the Cape Byron Light ❶, which for well over 100 years has warned ships off the Julian Rocks outcrop and enabled sailors to calibrate their location. Over half a million people from around the world visit it each year.

When you drive into Byron Bay, as most people do today, you are greeted with a sign insisting that you 'Cheer up, slow down, chill out'. Surfers, European backpackers, ageing hippies and fashion boutique shoppers crowd the streets. At night, many a venue hosts a band. The bourgeoisie live it up in expensive restaurants and those on a modest budget eat pizza in the street. My first visit, as a child on the annual family Christmas road trip from Melbourne to Brisbane in the 1950s, saw a run-down town with a couple of rough pubs and a whaling station. You could only escape the stench of the butchered whale carcasses by heading up to the lighthouse, built in 1901, where goats kept the grass down.

Until the 1960s, Byron Bay remained a dirty industrial town, with its piggery, abattoir and whaling station, its beaches given over to sand mining—a far cry from its reputation today as one of Australia's leading international and domestic tourism destinations. The traditional owners, the Arakwal people ❷, called the bay 'Cavanbah', or meeting place. Captain Cook found the bay to be a safe anchorage in 1770, and named it after an undistinguished naval commander John Byron, who came from the same aristocratic family as the poet Lord Byron.

Byron Bay is atypical of Australia's popular coastal resorts, in that it has only developed this reputation over the last 40 years, having almost no tourism before that. Many of our most well-known coastal holiday places were well established by the late nineteenth century, including Lorne, Sorrento and Queenscliff in Victoria, The Entrance and Coffs Harbour in New South Wales, Coolangatta on the

◄ Board riders at Byron in 2014. In the 1970s and 1980s, many board riders camped overnight in back streets in their VW vans or station wagons. Overnight camping proliferated with the rise of the backpacker market, and is now effectively banned with simple but readily enforceable signage, 'no parking 1am–5am'.

New South Wales–Queensland border, Glenelg and Victor Harbour in South Australia and Albany in Western Australia, which all boasted grand guesthouses.

Coastal towns with a rainforest hinterland usually started as ports for timber export. Byron Bay got its first boost from exporting, especially cedar, which was much prized for furniture making. Because the nearby Tweed and Richmond rivers needed expensive breakwaters to create safe shipping, Byron Bay proved the perfect site for the New South Wales government to build a jetty between 1886 and 1888 ❸. The spur railway arrived from Lismore in 1894, giving Byron a direct freight and passenger service to Sydney.

Mineral sand mining—for rutile and zircon—first took place in Australia on an industrial scale on the beach at Byron Bay in the mid-1930s. No-one complained in this rough industrial town, where the new industry provided much needed jobs, along with the abattoir, a cheese and milk factory and a piggery, which serviced hundreds of small dairy farms—themselves all created out of cleared rainforest land.

The sand mining ruined the beaches by chomping through the dunes and water blasting to sieve for the prized metals. Most of the demand came from the United States for use in steel alloys. Sand mining companies took over vast sections of the foreshore, from Bundaberg in Queensland to south of Sydney, paying state governments a modest leasing fee for what they termed 'black gold'. Getting rid of the black rutile from the beaches—remnants of which can still be seen on many east coast beaches—was promoted to the public as 'cleaning up the beach' by making the sand whiter. Later efforts by these companies to clean up the havoc they had caused on the coast, including planting South African 'bitou bush', with its yellow flower, proved disastrous, as the introduced species smothered the native coastal vegetation. For years, coastal councils have been spraying the bush in an attempt to eradicate it from the foreshores. Visitors often wonder why there is dead bush near the beach; few appreciate this continuing evidence of the environmental damage the mining caused.

Residents from inland country towns used Byron Bay as a summer escape, camping or building a fibro shack. Like many subtropical coastal towns, the February 1954 cyclone flooded the town centre, took much of the long jetty away

▼ Byron Bay still attracts hippies and ferals, however they are increasingly outnumbered by Australian and international holidaymakers.

and sunk the fishing fleet, the remnants relocating to a safer port to the immediate north at Brunswick Heads. Undeterred, the owner of the Byron Bay abattoir seized on this misfortune and established Australia's fifth whaling station in July 1954, appropriating what was left of the cyclone-damaged jetty. The whaling station, with an annual quota of 120 humpback whales, mainly destined for pet food, closed in 1962, not because of any protest, but because it had run out of whales to kill.

With the rapid growth of Sydney and Brisbane in the 1950s and 1960s, surfers found Byron Bay—with its magnificent beaches and iconic lighthouse—a laid-back and picturesque place to hang out. Overnight street camping in battered station wagons and VW vans became the order of the day. Longboard surfers embraced the peeling right-hand waves at 'The Pass' or the swell at 'The Wreck', named after the exposed wreck of SS *Wollongbar* 4. Byron became one of the key destinations for the burgeoning surf culture, with small surfboard manufacturing

▲ The whaling station at Byron Bay, established on the foreshortened wharf, closed in 1962, just eight years after it opened. They had run out of humpback whales to kill.

companies setting up shop. Young people taking time off at the end of high school or before commencing conventional employment would call in at major east-coast surfing sites, and Byron Bay became a must-visit, a lot more 'cool' than the increasingly commercialised Gold Coast. The Aquarius Festival held in Nimbin in 1973, some 75 kilometres north-west of Byron, brought with it a raft of alternative cultures, from yoga and Buddhism to umpteen varieties of spiritualism. The sweet smell of marijuana has wafted over the region ever since, most of it sourced from the nearby hinterland. The New South Wales Police still conduct raids, which *The Nimbin Good Times* monthly newspaper routinely denounces in favour of decriminalising marijuana.

Environmental battles over coastal rainforests, hotly fought in the 1970s and early 1980s, have produced some of the best-known protest campaigns in Australia, including Terania Creek, after whose champions the nearby Protesters Falls were named 5. Environmental activists lived to see a number of national parks created,

◄ The state government drew up plans for the Byron Bay lighthouse in the 1890s, and it opened in 1901. Automated in 1989, when the last lighthouse keeper left, the Byron Light is the most powerful in Australia.

▲ Byron Shire has a long history of activism, consistently rejecting over-development, as in this demonstration in 2004. In the nearby Gold Coast, a setting like this would already have been given over to high-rise apartments.

including Nightcap ⑥ and Jerusalem Creek Falls ⑦. Coastal heathland south of the lighthouse has, since 2001, been jointly managed by the Arakwal people and the New South Wales National Parks and Wildlife Service.

In 1986, the Australian actor Paul Hogan and his partner John Cornell released the film *Crocodile Dundee*, and Hogan became an international household name. In 1990, Cornell purchased and redeveloped the Beach Hotel ⑧ at Byron Bay and put the locality on the international tourism map. Today, Byron gets 1.7 million visitors a year, swamping its residential population.

Local residents have successfully fought to preserve not the original industrial character of the town—most of which has been obliterated—but its low-rise, relaxed character. The original piggery is now a cinema and boutique brewery ⑨. Staunch community opposition managed to fend off applications from Club Med for a huge tourist resort and from McDonalds for a hamburger joint. The council, headquartered in nearby Mullumbimby, is often dominated by 'green' councillors, who strive hard to maintain the natural setting, helped by the creation of a 12-kilometre marine reserve ⑩ north to Brunswick Heads by the state government. Of course, many local entrepreneurs still want to cash in, but there are no structures in the town higher than five stories. This is in stark contrast to the Gold Coast, just 60 kilometres north, where over 50 apartment blocks of between 20 and 80 storeys tower above the beach, casting long shadows over the few dunes that have survived from the days of sand mining there.

Since the establishment of the Blues Festival in 1990, the Byron Shire has become home to a plethora of festivals, from classical and rock music to books and alternative healing. Farmers' markets **11** are popular, while the Sunday market attracts over 100 store holders and customers to match. Byron Shire is one of the few smaller communities in Australia to retain a locally owned weekly newspaper, *The Byron Shire Echo*, founded in 1986. Fiercely independent, the *Echo* opposes coal seam gas mining and rock walls to protect wealthy residents who have built on the sand dunes of Belongil **12**, favours solar power and is always questioning the intentions of developers.

Tourism demand has placed enormous pressure on Byron, resulting in the introduction of paid parking for the first time in 2016. Two airports are nearby, Coolangatta and Ballina, and you can now drive from Brisbane to Byron on the freeway in under two hours. Most visitors are astonished to learn of the whaling and sand mining past, now well hidden by the brand name shops that crowd out the streets. The Brunswick Valley Historical Society Museum in Mullumbimby has a rich and varied collection of Byron's industrial past. Most visitors walk to the commanding lighthouse, as there is very little car parking. The lighthouse and its lighthouse keepers' cottages retain their original charm. It's a good spot to catch a glimpse of a passing whale from June to early September, when a replenished population of 15,000 humpback whales travels along the east coast heading north for warmer waters.

Explore the history

1 CAPE BYRON LIGHT
Lighthouse Rd

2 CAPE GALLERY OF ARAKWAL PEOPLE
Cape Byron Light, Lighthouse Rd

3 REMAINS OF JETTY
Belongil Beach

4 WRECK OF SS *WOLLONGBAR*
Main Beach, Johnson St

5 PROTESTERS FALLS
Terania Ck Rd, The Channon

6 NIGHTCAP NATIONAL PARK
Newton Dr, Nightcap

7 JERUSALEM CREEK FALLS
Barrington Tops National Park

8 BEACH HOTEL
1 Bay St

9 BYRON BAY BREWERY (OLD PIGGERY)
1 Skinners Shoot Rd

10 JULIAN ROCKS MARINE RESERVE

11 BYRON FARMERS' MARKET
Butler St Reserve

12 BELONGIL BEACH

The Cowra Breakout

Vol. V. No. 39   *Telephone: M2406*   SYDNEY, SUNDAY, AUGUST 6, 1944   Registered at the G.P.O., Sydney, for transmission by post as a newspaper.   Price 3

WAR PRISONERS ESCAPE FROM CAMP

Wide search by troops, police

From Our Special Representative

Armed soldiers and civilian police are scouring the Cowra district for prisoners of war who escaped yesterday morning.

The men broke away from the prisoner-of-war camp near Cowra at 2 a.m.

Residents in homesteads and isolated districts have been warned to keep their children and womenfolk indoors at night.

Some prisoners have been recaptured by police and soldiers.

By nightfall others were reported to have reached points 10 to 15 miles from Cowra.

They were moving in different directions.

People living in and near Cowra were warned yesterday in a special broadcast that the escapees might attempt to secure assistance

They were told to inform military or police authorities if they were approached by escapees, and to keep a sharp watch for strangers.

The number of prisoners who escaped from the camp or their nationality has not been announced.

They carefully planned their escape by first setting fire to their huts and running out into the open compound.

They carried blankets and clothing and threw these over the barbed-wire entanglements to break them down and climb over.

The alarm was given and the Australian guards rushed to stop the escaping prisoners.

Guards On Roads

"We approached cautiously, but found the prisoners quite mild.

"After we had captured them we found they were armed with knives. Constables McGovern and Cooper also recaptured another escapee during the day.

Tonight I spoke to Mrs. Walter Weir, who "entertained" three of the escaped prisoners at morning tea.

Mrs. Weir lives beside her sister-in-law, Mrs. Robert Weir, at Homewood, six miles out of Cowra.

Mrs. Weir said that three prisoners had apparently slept in the woolshed during the night and emerged soon after breakfast.

"They came up to the house about 9.30," she said.

"They were first seen by my little girl, Margaret, aged 15. She was very frightened.

Well-behaved

"My husband was down in the cattle paddock at the time.

"The prisoners were well behaved, friendly, and sat down on the side verandah.

"I got them scones and tea, which

thanked us and returned to the woolshed also.

"Soon afterwards military police arrived and took the prisoners in charge."

Prime Minister Curtin, who is in Melbourne, and Army Minister Forde, who is in Queensland, were immediately informed of the escapes.

Before full particulars of escapes of prisoners of war can be published, an official Governmental report must be made to the enemy country concerned.

This report, under international agreement, is made through the consular representative of the protecting Power.

New Zealand Escape

A number of war prisoners have escaped in ones and twos from Australian prison camps during this war.

At Featherston, New Zealand, in February last year, 48 Japanese prisoners of war were killed or died of wounds during a riot in a prison camp.

In an official statement New Zealand Prime Minister Fraser said the riot began when Japanese prisoners

Nazis Pack Roads

ALLIED ARMIES PUSH ON

GUERNSEY   JERSEY   CHERBOURG   LE HAVRE   ST LO   CAEN   AUNAY   VIRE   ST.POIS   MORTAIN   ALENCON   BREST   ST. MALO   DINAN   LOUDEAC   QUIMPER   PONTIVY   RENNES   LAVAL   LE MANS   LORIENT   PIPRIAC   CHATEAUBRIANT   VANNES   REDON   DERVAL   ANGERS   NANTES   LOIRE   TOURS   ST. NAZAIRE   20   40   60 Miles

Allies move swiftly on French ports

SUNDAY TELEGRAPH SERVICE AND AAP

LONDON, Sat.—American forces thrusting south in France are expected to reach St. Nazaire and cut off the whole Brittany Peninsula by tomorrow.

U.S. spearheads today advanced 18 miles in five hours to Pipriac and Derval.

They are now only 30 miles from the coast.

Their advance threatens to cut off thousands of German troops in the tip of the peninsula.

Capture of the peninsula will give the Allies the great ports at Brest, Lorient, and St. Malo, as well as those at St. Nazaire and Nantes.

Already the B.B.C. reports fighting in St. Malo.

The Germans are throwing in Tiger tanks in an attempt to prevent the Americans reaching the port.

Another American force is pushing up the peninsula towards Brest.

But the most important U.S. drive continues to be from the great road and rail terminus of Rennes (captured on Thursday) towards the Loire River.

Allied forces from Rennes are within artillery range of both St. Nazaire, at the mouth of the Loire, and Nantes, big river port.

"The 'bomb-line' is the safety line between our own and enemy troops.

"The Army told the Air Force 'just bomb where you can see Germans.'

"So our planes are sweeping down to tree-top height to identify our transport from the enemy's.

"Fortunately flying weather is ideal and it is not difficult to select nice fat German targets for nice fat British bombs."

E. W. Macalpine, Sunday Telegraph London Editor, says:

"The Americans are roaming through Brittany Peninsula almost at will.

"The only determined and organised section of the German front seems to be opposite the British. Opposite the Americans there is no indication of any determined co-ordinated resistance of any line on which the Germans might stand.

"They may attempt to regroup in country south of a line running roughly from Fougeres to Argentan, but most probably they will have to retire

Hundreds of Japanese soldiers broke out of the Cowra Prisoner of War Camp in August 1944, the largest mass escape of prisoners in modern military history. It is an unusual claim to fame for an inland Australian country town. The camp is a reminder of the bitterness that war creates, but it also demonstrates the prospects for reconciliation, with Japanese and Australian war dead lying in adjoining graveyards. In a serene garden setting, the nearby Japanese Garden and Cultural Centre promotes understanding and respect for a very different culture.

Cowra is a popular place to visit in autumn, because its deciduous trees add great colour to its undulating landscape. If you are driving from Canberra or Sydney, one of the first things that greets you on the outskirts of town, apart from garish advertisements for fast food franchises, is a series of signs pointing to the Japanese war cemetery, the Prisoner of War camp and the Japanese Garden. Many travellers stop at the cemetery first, where, when entering the Japanese section, they are confronted by some hundreds of plaques for war dead. What is unusual about this cemetery is that many of the people buried here died in the largest Prisoner of War (POW) escape in modern military history.

The Australian army established 28 POW camps during the Second World War, which housed Australian residents who were deemed a threat to national security, including Italians and Germans, as well as prisoners captured by Australian troops in Africa. The Cowra camp had four 17-acre compounds, designed to hold 1,000 prisoners each. Some were internees, including Javanese and other Indonesians handed to Australia by Dutch authorities. The inmates were surrounded by barbed-wire fences and large observation towers overlooking the perimeter. By 1944, two camps held Italian POWs, one held Korean and Formosan POWs and Japanese officers, and the remaining camp contained 1,104 Japanese POWs. The Japanese POWs were much more resentful than any of the other groups who did not suffer the same sense of national disgrace on capture. Some POWs sought day work outside the camp, but not the Japanese.

On 4 August 1944, to relieve overcrowding, the army decided to move all Japanese below the rank of lance corporal to the POW camp at Hay, 400 kilometres west. The Japanese POWs were angry at the prospective move, and formed a plan to escape. A bugle call at 1.50am on 5 August from Hajime Toyoshima—a Zero pilot captured during the first bombing attack on Darwin—signalled the start of the breakout. Hundreds of Japanese from Compound B attacked the perimeter wire in four places. Armed with knives and any other implements they could lay their hands on, including baseball gloves and blankets to place over the barbed wire, 378 managed to escape, 334 fleeing into the nearby countryside.

◄ Wartime censorship meant that it took some time for newspaper readers in Australia to find out just how many Japanese prisoners had escaped from the Cowra camp. This newspaper account indicates that escapees were well behaved at a nearby homestead, offered morning tea and later peacefully apprehended by military police.

Blankets were thrown over barbed wire in B compound by prisoners to aid their escape. Security arrangements were rather minimal, as it had not occurred to the authorities that an escape attempt would be made, especially on such a scale.

► Knives and other improvised weapons found in and near B compound immediately after the 'mass escape'. These relics are now held by the Australian War Memorial.

One officer and 233 rank-and-file soldiers were killed, mainly by machine-gun fire, or died of self-inflicted wounds, as Japanese military culture held that it was a disgrace to both family and nation to be taken prisoner. Many had not informed their families in Japan that they were in a POW camp for this reason.

Twenty buildings, including accommodation huts, were burnt. Three Australian guards died in the fighting, another in the round up. The 'Cowra breakout', as it soon came to be known, remains the largest mass escape of POWs in modern military history; only 76 Allied prisoners managed the 'Great Escape' from Stalag Luft III in Germany in March 1944.

The Australian and Japanese war cemeteries are established side by side. Impressed at the way the local RSL cares for the cemeteries, the Japanese government decided, in 1963, to relocate all other Japanese war dead buried in Australia to the Cowra cemetery. The cemetery itself gets Japanese visitors, and flowers are regularly laid at some of the graves. In 2014, Mami Yamada, who wrote a doctoral thesis based on interviews with Japanese POW survivors, visited Cowra with one of the remaining survivors, then aged 93. She noted that the breakout is rarely mentioned in mainstream Japanese accounts of the Second World War.

For some time now, the main tourist brochure on Cowra has been subtitled 'the great escape'. In the 2016 edition, the front cover depicted not the remnant POW camp but retirees enjoying the Japanese Garden. After taking in the history, the setting and the tragedy of the breakout, the visitor can drive or walk along a cherry tree-lined avenue to the Japanese Garden, established in 1979 to further develop the relationship between the people of Cowra and the people of Japan. Five hectares of hillside, including waterfalls, streams and lakes, designed by Ken Nakajima, create as the brochure claims 'a tranquil and serene environment for visitors all year round'. Popular with locals as a place for morning or afternoon tea, the garden has become a tourist destination in its own right. Japan is a land of deciduous trees and ample water, and the plantings reflect these elements. Beyond the lush borders of the garden, the dry environment of the Australian bush—gum trees and grass tussocks—is just like the setting of the POW camp. A recently created 'Garrison Trail' leads visitors back to the POW site, where elaborate signage about the site's history, much of it funded from Japan, explains the events that unfolded in August 1944.

You can't forget the breakout when you continue your journey through the Cowra township, especially when you encounter the 'Breakout Motel'.

▼ The Japanese penchant for serene, manicured gardens is evident in the plantings, design and structures of the Japanese Garden in Cowra.

Myall Creek Massacre

There were over 150 massacres of Aboriginal people in Australia between 1794 and 1872. Some are well documented, but most are not. In the 1990s, there was a concerted attempt by some politicians and writers to downplay the extent of frontier violence, dismissing some historians as purveyors of 'black armband history'. In the biggest massacre, at Slaughterhouse Creek, not far from Myall Creek, 300 Aboriginal people were killed, and none of the 15 heavily armed stockmen who attacked the Wirrayaraay people in a dawn raid were charged. But at Myall Creek, just a few weeks later, the perpetrators were tried for murder and seven were executed. Travellers can now visit a memorial to this massacre, unveiled on 10 June 2000.

Equidistant between the townships of Bingara and Delungra, the Myall Creek Massacre and Memorial Site is 30 kilometres south-west of Inverell, 450 kilometres from Brisbane and 580 kilometres from Sydney. The site itself is well signposted, but it is not on a major highway, and doesn't feature on any bus tours. Most visitors are curious travellers who follow the sign to the memorial and may or may not know about the massacre before visiting. Around 30 Indigenous people were murdered here in June 1838, in one of the most documented massacres in Australia, not least because it is the first one where some of the white perpetrators were tried and hanged. Visitors can record their thoughts in a visitors' book, and for many the scale and brutality of the massacre comes as a shock.

A 500-metre track through the bush leads to the Myall Creek Memorial. Seven plaques set in granite boulders explain what happened on 10 June 1838, in English and in the Gamilaraay language. Some historic sites are always in the public eye, but others such as this fade from common knowledge, only to re-emerge at anniversaries, or when local populations reflect on the history of their region.

In 1837, Henry Dangar established the Myall Creek Station, part of his growing pastoral empire. Clashes between Europeans, many of convict origin, and Indigenous people were common, and in January 1838 up to 50 Aboriginal people died in battles with police in Waterloo Creek, near the Namoi and Gwydir rivers. In May, Charles Kilmeister, one of the convict station hands at the Myall Creek property, invited about 50 members of the local Wirrayaraay nation to camp there. On the morning of Monday 10 June, ten of the group's able-bodied men had gone to a neighbouring station to cut bark. About 4pm that day, at least ten stockmen herded the remaining Wirrayaraay people—about 30, including women and children—into the workmen's hut. The hut keeper George Anderson refused to join the group and stayed at a different hut with four young Aboriginal people: two Peel River lads who had been released; one boy who had escaped; and a girl who had been 'given' to Anderson. The stockmen took the rest of the group a few

◄ This photograph, taken in 1921, represents Myall Creek as a typical outback bush landscape, with no visible evidence—and no reminder —of the atrocity committed here.

This image, created by Camden Pelham, shows Aboriginal people being captured and 'slaughtered' by convicts. The images appeared in *The Chronicles of Crime* (1891), aimed at a crime-hungry British audience.

hundred metres away and hacked and slashed them to death. One of the Peel River boys, 'Davey', spied on the scene and brought back the terrible news. Property superintendent William Hobbs, who had been away at the time, returned to the station to discover separated heads and bodies, which the stockmen had attempted, unsuccessfully, to burn. Hobbs reported the incident to his employer, Dangar. Hearing of the massacre, a nearby landholder wrote about the incident to Governor Gipps. When the investigating police party finally got to the site, it had been cleaned up, with only small children's bones to be found.

Gipps had been the governor of New South Wales for just four months. The British government had issued him with instructions to protect the colony's Indigenous inhabitants, as members of the House of Commons had expressed grave concerns about their maltreatment. Gipps sent a party of mounted police to investigate, and gradually the suspects were identified, including Kilmeister. Eleven men went to trial on 15 November. They were acquitted by the jury within 15 minutes—with much cheering in the court from a supportive crowd—because there was a lack of physical evidence. The prosecution based its case around the murder of 'Daddy', a Wirrayaraay Elder, but his remains had been destroyed. Attorney-General Plunkett successfully moved for a second trial, which focused on the remains of a child. Dangar contributed to the prisoners' defence fund and

The Avengers (1860) by the artist Samuel Thomas Gill. Recent research on massacres indicates that less than ten per cent of recorded conflicts involved Indigenous people killing settlers.

supported Kilmeister at the trial, saying he was of good character, while attacking the character of Anderson, a witness for the prosecution. Attempts by the defence to discredit Anderson failed, and on his testimony, along with the testimony of others including Hobbs and a dentist who could identify some of the bones and teeth as those of a child, Kilmeister and six other men were convicted and executed on 18 December 1838.

The Sydney Morning Herald sided with the perpetrators, not the victims:

We want neither the classic nor the romantic savage here. We have far too many of the murderous wretches about us already … The whole gang of black animals are not worth the money the colonists will have to pay for printing the silly court documents on which we have already wasted too much time.

This was the first time that white men were arrested and hanged for the massacre of Indigenous Australians. Such massacres were rarely mentioned in school textbooks, which until the last 50 years glossed over dispossession, treating the nation's first peoples as quaint and backward. The extent of dispossession has only gradually entered broader public consciousness, as notable scholars including Charles Rowley and Henry Reynolds began documenting Aboriginal resistance, the many battles and massacres, and the impact of European diseases.

In January 1965, Len Payne, a Bingara resident, suggested a memorial to those who had been murdered at Myall Creek. He gained little support, with another resident denouncing the idea as 'an insult to the Bingara people'. Payne tried but failed to get support from the Apex club.

The Uniting Church held a conference on reconciliation at Myall Creek in 1998 and a memorial committee was set up. Two years later, the committee unveiled a memorial, which brought together descendants of the victims, survivors and, unusually, perpetrators of the massacre. In 2008, the site was added to the National Heritage List.

After walking along the track and reading the plaques, you arrive at the memorial to read the inscription:

In memory of the Wirrayaraay People who were murdered on the slopes of this ridge in an unprovoked but premeditated act in the late afternoon of 10 June 1838.
Erected on 10 June 2000 by a group of Aboriginal and non-Aboriginal Australians in an act of reconciliation, and in acknowledgement of the truth of our shared history.
We remember them. Ngiyani winangay ganunga.

◄ The Myall Creek memorial, unveiled in 2000, is a stark reminder of the massacre.

Nutcote: Home of May Gibbs

Take a turn in the harbourside cottage garden at Nutcote, where children's author and illustrator May Gibbs lived for 44 years, and you can very easily imagine a pair of gumnut babies—her signature image—scurrying out of sight behind a shrub or a rose. Gibbs walked in her garden with notebook and pencil, jotting down ideas and images for new characters and stories. Nutcote has been beautifully restored with late 1920s furnishings, its modest dimensions a refreshing reminder that Sydney Harbour wasn't always colonised by the oversized mansions of the rich.

When you look out at the waters of Neutral Bay from May Gibbs' house Nutcote, you see in the middle distance the arch of the Sydney Harbour Bridge. Built for the children's book author and illustrator in 1925, Nutcote's front verandah gave Gibbs a perfect view of the construction of the bridge from the arches rising from both sides of the harbour to its completion in March 1932.

Both of May Gibbs' parents were art students in Britain. They migrated to Australia in the early 1880s. With two sons and one daughter, they settled in Perth, where May's father continued to paint and draw cartoons, and became a surveyor. May returned to England between 1901 and 1904 where she studied at various art schools, and again between 1909 and 1913, when she undertook illustrations for publishers and magazines, and illustrated a fantasy book on London chimneys. Advised by her doctor to return to Australia for health reasons, she lived in boarding houses in Neutral Bay, and often travelled in to Circular Quay by ferry. She earned her living by sketching soldiers about to leave for the war and drawing magazine covers, including for *The Lone Hand* and *The Sydney Mail*.

Fascinated by Australian flora and fauna, her first Gumnut book was published in 1916. She specialised in botanically accurate drawings, skilfully creating gumnut and blossom babies, as well as evil Banksia men. Her book *Snugglepot and Cuddlepie*, published in 1918, became an overnight success. Her popularity saw her commissioned to undertake a weekly Sunday newspaper cartoon strip *Bib and Bub*, which ran from 1924 to 1967, just five years before she died.

After her marriage in Perth in 1919, she returned with her husband, a mining agent, to Neutral Bay. Her parents helped her buy a waterfront block of land, and in 1924 architect B.J. Waterhouse designed for them a modest Mediterranean-style house featuring elegant stained timberwork, which he dubbed 'Nutcote'. May took continual inspiration from her garden, as she explained in an interview recorded for the National Library's Oral History collection:

▼ May Gibbs has captivated children with her drawings and stories for a hundred years. Many of her books are still in print.

◄ While Nutcote has changed little since 1925, first the Harbour Bridge and later high-rise apartment blocks now dominate its harbour outlook.

it's a dear little place with a long, long garden, in which I wandered about and would pull weeds and dig for plants and I'm very fond of it … trees top and bottom and all round and plenty of grass and birds.

She continued to work on illustrated children's books for the next three decades, but plans for overseas publication and film rights didn't materialise, partly because the Great Depression made publishers more circumspect.

May bequeathed Nutcote to UNICEF, who in 1970 auctioned off the contents and later sold the property to a developer, who then rented it. At that time, Heritage Councils were being established in all states, and there was a growing awareness that most historic houses that had been saved were grand establishments that reflected the lives of great men, rarely of women. Classified by the New South Wales branch of the National Trust in 1986, a campaign to save Nutcote began the following year. In 1988, the New South Wales Heritage Council placed a permanent conservation order on the house, but neither the state nor the federal government would advance funds for its purchase as a house museum. To its great credit, the North Sydney Council purchased the property in 1991, and since 1994 it has been open to the public as a modest historic house and a garden museum. Nutcote contains original furnishings and some of May's paintings, books, sketches and newspaper columns, as well as family photographs. It is a charming memorial to the work of May Gibbs, a notable writer and illustrator of children's books.

The LONE HAND

CHRISTMAS
NUMBER

PRICE SIXPENCE

The Sydney Opera House

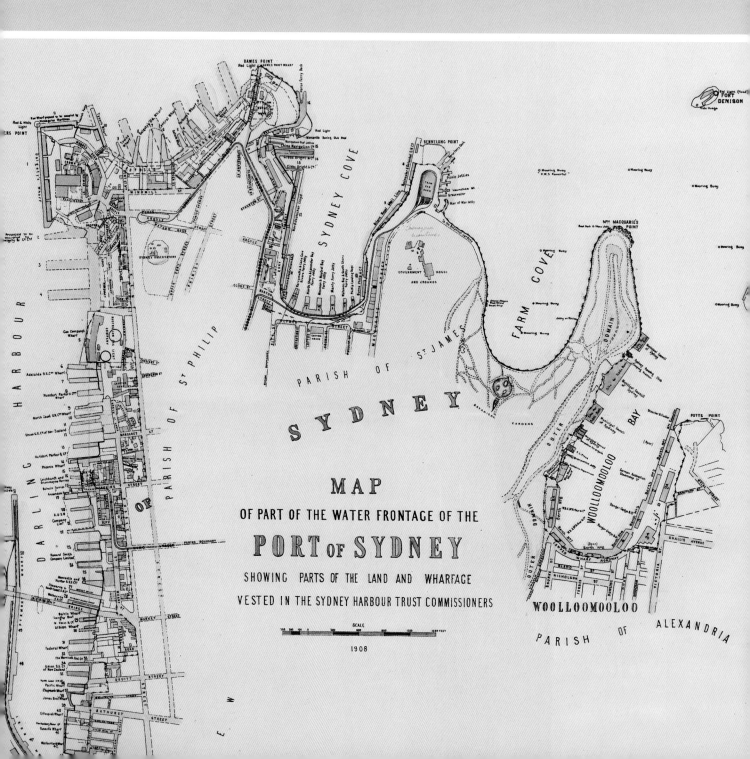

MAP

OF PART OF THE WATER FRONTAGE OF THE

PORT OF SYDNEY

SHOWING PARTS OF THE LAND AND WHARFAGE

VESTED IN THE SYDNEY HARBOUR TRUST COMMISSIONERS

SCALE

1908

The Sydney Opera House is the only Australian structure that is instantly recognised around the world. And, it is one of just a handful of twentieth-century buildings to be inscribed on UNESCO's World Heritage List. With his white shell-shaped sails, Danish architect Jørn Utzon brilliantly capitalised on a superb harbourside site. The Sydney fireworks, featuring the Sydney Harbour Bridge and the Opera House, command a huge international television audience each year.

An opera house, primarily offering high art, is a surprising contender for the most recognisable structure of a former British convict colony, founded on the dispossession of its original inhabitants. Located on Bennelong Point, named after the Aboriginal man befriended and promoted by the first English Governor of New South Wales, Arthur Phillip, the Opera House enjoys a commanding position on Sydney Harbour.

How is it that a prospective opera house could, in mid-1950s Sydney, be offered such a magnificent site? The answer is twofold. In 1817, Governor Lachlan Macquarie had his architect Francis Greenway, a former convict, design a fort to protect Sydney from naval invasion. Fort Macquarie's castellated tower and circular bastions, all in stone, housed 15 canons. With the construction and expansion of naval defences at Middle Head, where long-range canons could be trained on the

▼ The Opera House and the Harbour Bridge are Australia's best-known structures, beamed around the world for the New Year's Eve fireworks.

◀ This 1908 map shows the Tram Shed in pride of place on Bennelong Point. Longshore freight wharves lined both sides of Sydney Cove, while ferries took passengers as far afield as Manly and the Parramatta River.

▶ Freight ships wait to dock
and a ferry steams to Manly
behind Bennelong Point
and the Tram Shed in this
1958 image.

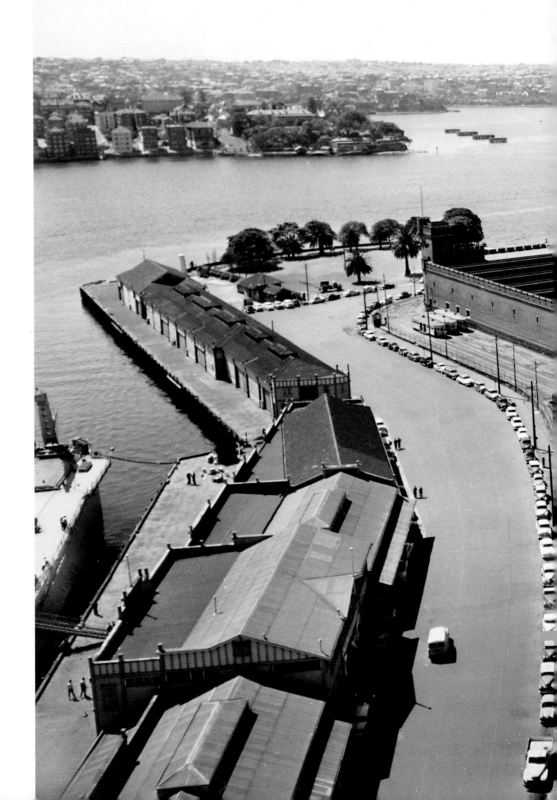

entrance to Sydney Harbour, Fort Macquarie became redundant for defence purposes. Demolished in 1901, the site soon housed the purpose-built Fort Macquarie Tram Depot, the centrepiece of Australia's largest tramway system.

Circular Quay had long been a maritime hub. In the 1830s, the colonial government sold off land on the eastern side to commercial shipping firms, and from the 1850s passenger and later vehicular ferries plied the north shore. When the New South Wales government decided to abandon trams in favour of buses in the early 1950s, it followed the precedent set in other major cities, especially in the United States and Britain. The Fort Macquarie Tram Depot was pronounced redundant, just like its military predecessor.

The Royal Australian Institute of Architects lauded the state government's decision to anoint Bennelong Point as the site for its 'national opera house', thrown open to international competition in 1956. As the architects saw it, 'the occupation of this conspicuous headland, so near the heart of the city, by a tram shed, is an absurdity'. Few regretted the demolition of the Fort Macquarie Tram Depot.

▼ The Opera House was nearing completion in 1967, with the sails already in place. For well over a decade, millions of ferry passengers saw it take shape.

Getting rid of old-fashioned trams and replacing them with buses would make Sydney a modern city. Circular Quay—run-down, dirty, full of warehouses and rough pubs—and the nearby 'Rocks', which was home to maritime workers, needed to be cleaned up. East Circular Quay, today home to multi-million-dollar apartments, housed ageing warehouses and non-descript offices.

Two hundred and thirty-three entries were received from architects around the world for the competition to design the opera house, with the Danish architect Jørn Utzon's scheme announced the winner in January 1957. Proud of Utzon's distinctive design, replete with concrete sails covered in white tiles, the state Labor government claimed in its celebratory brochure in March 1959 that:

> when the great ocean liners come through the Heads and round Bradley's Point, a new landmark will welcome visitors and home-coming Australians will look eagerly for the white sails of the Opera House roofs against the green background of the Botanic Gardens and the Domain.

The unusual shape, happily played with by cartoonists, provided a constant source of newspaper fodder as technical difficulties and cost overruns were trumpeted in the press. Some of the cost was met by the Opera House Lottery. Utzon was forced to resign as Chief Architect in 1966, amid bitter controversy. He never returned to Australia.

The white sails gradually arose over the vast granite podium at Bennelong Point, keeping the city captivated. Earlier generations of Sydneysiders recalled how they had marvelled at the building of the Harbour Bridge, its gaunt steel arch now juxtaposed with an explicitly modern structure.

When opened by Queen Elizabeth II in 1973, few imagined that four decades later over eight million people a year would visit the Opera House. There is no entry fee, but to get into the Concert Hall, the Opera Theatre or the other venues, you have to pay for a guided tour or be attending a performance, and one and a half million people a year do just that.

▲ Architect Jørn Utzon's model of the geometry of the Sydney Opera House's shells instantly conveyed his innovative design.

Go by Train to ‒

CENTRAL AUSTRALIA

FOR WINTER HOLIDAYS

Northern Territory

Darwin

Darwin is the only Australian city ever to be destroyed twice in its history. Rained with more bombs than Pearl Harbor in 1942, hundreds died, mainly on naval ships in the harbour. Three decades later, nature rent its fury, destroying thousands of homes that had been built to house a growing population. Darwin, the capital of the Northern Territory, has become a flamboyant and quirky place, known for its casual outlook and croc stories that challenge even the most gullible. The night markets of Darwin are testament to the cosmopolitan mix of the population, offering food from around the globe, and both international and local Indigenous arts and crafts. As it is always hot and humid, both locals and visitors are often found sitting on the beach watching the sun set over the Arafura Sea.

At the very top of Australia is the small, isolated city of Darwin, 1,489 kilometres from Alice Springs and 3,042 kilometres from the next capital city, Adelaide. Like many cities that have been damaged by war or natural disasters, there is little in Darwin's present landscape to indicate Japanese bombing raids between 1942 and 1943, or the fury of Cyclone Tracy on Christmas Day 1974. Today, the heart of the city is home to an elegant tropical Parliament House ❶, a casino ❷ overlooking the Arafura Sea and scores of medium- and high-rise apartment buildings, all built to withstand cyclones. Like other Australian tropical cities, stingers and the threat of crocodiles, alongside Darwin's big tidal variations, mean that swimming is confined to public and private pools. A recently reclaimed Waterfront tourist zone ❸ boasts a wave pool and an urban beach, beyond the reach of crocodiles. But to most visitors being told that you can't go swimming in the inviting ocean comes as a shock. Imagine the relief on hearing that Kakadu, the nation's largest national park, contains pools where you can safely take a dip.

Opposite the new Waterfront precinct is the entrance to oil storage tunnels ❹ built in the Second World War. Here we learn that the federal government had been building up naval defences since 1938, including fuel storage. No-one, not least the Japanese army and navy, ever imagined that their invasion of south-east Asia would proceed so quickly. Just as the British never thought that Singapore might fall, the Australian authorities never anticipated that Darwin might be attacked by air rather than by sea ❺. Ten weeks after the attack on Pearl Harbor, and four days after the fall of Singapore, on 19 February 1942 188 aircraft from Japanese aircraft carriers in the Timor Sea, and another 54 land-based bombers, killed 235 American and Australian military personnel and a number of civilians. Attacks continued on Darwin and other northern towns until November 1943. All the oil storage facilities were above ground and readily

◄ Oil storage tanks go up in flames after being hit by the first Japanese air raid on Darwin in 1942.

◄ Most of Darwin has been built or rebuilt in the 45 years since the cyclone. Government offices jostle with apartment blocks. Much of the foreshore has been replanted and made accessible to the public, safe for walkers, but not for swimmers.

destroyed, while Australian and American ships, including destroyers retreating from the Philippines, were an easy target.

Hajime Toyoshima, a Zero pilot who had also been at Pearl Harbor, crash-landed on Melville Island, just north of Darwin, providing the first intact Zero plane taken by the Allies. Disarmed by local Aboriginal men, he became the first POW ever taken on Australian soil. Subsequently sent to the Cowra POW camp, his bugle call sounded the start of the Japanese outbreak there on 5 August 1944. Like many others, he committed suicide rather than be recaptured. His remains are in the Japanese war cemetery at Cowra, and the bugle is now in the collection of the Australian War Memorial.

Much of the population of Darwin—especially women and children—was evacuated after the bombing of Pearl Harbor. The local newspaper reported daily on the Japanese advance in south-east Asia, and the sinking of a Japanese submarine near Darwin Harbour on 20 January 1942. After the 19 February bombing, Darwin effectively came under military rule, with more evacuations. With the build-up of American troops aimed at dislodging the Japanese from New Guinea and south-east Asia, Darwin became home not only to the troops themselves but to military hospitals and a bevy of airstrips, some of which can still be seen today abutting major roads out of the city.

Darwin is hot and humid the year round, especially in summer. Until the coming of air conditioning, most Darwin residences were houses on concrete stilts, with fibro, louvred windows and fans, and iron roofs. These houses were lightweight and suited the climate, but few withstood the onslaught of Cyclone Tracy ❻ on Christmas Day 1974. Darwin had experienced less severe cyclones in 1897 and 1937 but these had long faded from memory. Although the Bureau of Meteorology issued warnings of a cyclone to the north of the city, few anticipated its severity nor its 217-kilometre per hour winds, which disabled the bureau's own measuring device. Fifty-three people were killed in the city and another 13 lost their lives at sea, mainly in boats in the harbour. Over half the city's homes were destroyed and another fifth suffered severe damage. Roofing iron and fibro sheeting flew through the air. Many people sheltered in their bathrooms, rooms that survived when the rest of the house collapsed. Even substantial stone buildings, including the Anglican Cathedral, succumbed to the ferocity of the wind. Telecommunications, power, water and sewerage systems all ceased to function.

The buildings that survived intact were multi-storey buildings in the city centre, built of concrete and reinforced steel, and most of the two-storey walk-up blocks of flats built of bèsser blocks. The question of why buildings, especially houses, did or did not survive was a major focus of research for the Darwin Reconstruction Commission, set up by the federal government just two months after the cyclone hit. By then, 25,000 people had left by air, many in troop planes, and 12,000 residents

▲ Japanese bombers attacked both American and Australian naval ships in Darwin harbour, where most of the city's deaths occurred.

▶ Franck Gohier's screen print *Darwin 1942* is based on a historical photograph of the wreckage of a Japanese Zero plane outside a bombed Darwin barracks.

Most houses in the suburb of Casuarina were destroyed by the cyclone. Lynn John Cox returned from his holiday to find his Holden car a ruin and his house a wreck, memorably recorded in this photograph by Bruce Howard.

had gone south in their own cars. The city's population fell from 47,000 to just over 10,000, with mainly men remaining. For six months after the cyclone, a permit system regulated access to the city, not least because authorities feared abandoned homes and businesses would be looted. Survivors of the 1942 bombing noticed a number of similarities between life in Darwin then and life after Cyclone Tracy.

Darwin has experienced three great exoduses in its history: the first after the Japanese attack on Pearl Harbor; the second after the first and largest of the Japanese bombing raids on the city itself; and the third after Cyclone Tracy. The city has been rebuilt twice, first after the bombing, and then after the cyclone, which heralded new building regulations. Many of these new building regulations, including steel rods linking ceiling bearers to floor bearers, also trickled down to other parts of Australia prone to severe storm damage.

In recent years, the central business district and its water-view surrounds have been redeveloped, almost beyond recognition, with 8- to 33-storey apartment blocks. This investor-led apartment boom, in a city that only has a population of 120,000, is predicated on future grand expectations. Half of the working population is in Territory and federal government employment in education, health and defence. And almost half of all Territorians rent their dwellings, so many workers and families only stay for a few years. Ten per cent of Darwin's population is Indigenous, and perhaps a third of this group consists of occasional visitors, coming in from the remote settlements in Arnhem Land and other parts of the Territory. Despite its proximity to Asia, Darwin has more British-born residents than any other foreign group, with Filipinos making up the next largest group. It used to have a substantial Greek and Chinese population, but that has been on the wane for some time. Backpackers flock to Darwin, where the combination of a perennially warm climate and open-air bars proves a great attraction. By late afternoon, drinking beer provides relief from the heat.

The city and the inner suburbs retain some notable structures from prewar defences and the war, including two massive rotating long-range cannons to repulse an attack from the sea. The recently completed Darwin Military Museum ❼ is designed around some remnant military defences, giving it rather more immediacy than many military memorials. You can visit the huge oil storage tunnels excavated into the hill (on which Parliament House now stands) in 1943. They never saw enemy action because, by the time they were ready for use, the Japanese were retreating in New Guinea and elsewhere in south-east Asia.

No other cities in Australia have been rebuilt twice in their history. In the case of Darwin, these episodes of rebuilding and repopulating were just 30 years apart. But to get any immediate sense of either the bombing or the cyclone, you have to visit the excellent displays at both the Northern Territory ❽ and the Military museums. Locals and tourists alike regularly gather at nearby Mindil Beach ❾ to see the sun set over the Arafura Sea and experience the vibrancy of the evening markets.

Explore the history

❶ **PARLIAMENT HOUSE**
State Square, Mitchell St

❷ **CASINO**
Gilruth Ave, The Gardens

❸ **DARWIN WATERFRONT PRECINCT**

❹ **WWII OIL STORAGE TANKS**
Kitchener Dr

❺ **DEFENCE OF DARWIN EXPERIENCE**
Alec Fong Lim Dr, East Point

❻ **CYCLONE TRACY ROOM AT MUSEUM AND ART GALLERY OF NORTHERN TERRITORY**
Bullocky Point

❼ **DARWIN MILITARY MUSEUM**
Alec Fong Lim Dr, East Point

❽ **MUSEUM AND ART GALLERY OF NORTHERN TERRITORY**
Bullocky Point

❾ **MINDIL BEACH AND MARKETS**

The Ghan

A rail link between Adelaide and Darwin was desired for well over a century, the need for a reliable supply of water and the vagaries of nature dictating both tempo and course. Conceived before Federation, the last stretch to Darwin didn't open until 2003. Now, it has become a sought-after traveller experience and one of the great train journeys of the world. Named for the Afghan cameleers who carried wares along the route, the railway's 2,979 kilometres afford ample time to reflect on the remoteness of the outback and the challenges faced by the region's inhabitants—past and present. The distant dream of a north–south freight link to the port of Darwin finally became a reality, so Australia can now boast two transcontinental lines, the first east–west, the second north–south.

Until the coming of the railway, the only practical way to get from one side of Australia to the other was by ship. Trains could move both people and goods across large landmasses, linking inland settlements and port cities. Transcontinental rail networks caught the popular imagination in the last decades of the nineteenth century, with railways planned to cross the United States, Canada, Australia, Asia and Europe. These were immense distances, which took horse-drawn vehicles many months to undertake.

The South Australian government had long sought a north–south transcontinental railway from Darwin to Adelaide, opening up the prospect of shipping links to Asia and Europe. But the Western Australian Premier John Forrest got in first, backing the east–west transcontinental railway as one way of encouraging Western Australians to vote in favour of federation. That railway route would link Sydney and Broken Hill to Kalgoorlie and Perth, but would also be readily accessible from Adelaide. The South Australian government had to content itself with starting a narrow-gauge railway from Port Augusta to Alice Springs. It took ten years to get to Oodnadatta (1881–1891) and then stalled. The Overland Telegraph Line had already mapped out the route in 1872, linking Australia with the world by above-ground and then undersea cable. Transport along this route had been the preserve of Afghan cameleers, their mule trains vital to the construction of the line. After the opening of the first section of the railway, they continued to ply their trade from Oodnadatta to Alice Springs.

In the *Northern Territory Acceptance Act 1910*, South Australia handed over the northern portion of the state to the new Commonwealth government, to create the Northern Territory. Part of the sweetener was that the Commonwealth would construct a railway from the port of Darwin to the South Australian border. That didn't happen, but the Commonwealth did extend the South Australian track northwards so it finally got to Alice Springs in 1929. The Adelaide *Advertiser* of

◀ Residents of Alice Springs admire the mighty locomotive in 1954.

◀ The many carriages of the Ghan, with its bright red diesel engine, cut a swathe through the timeless landscape of central Australia.

▲ A publicity logo produced for the inaugural Adelaide to Darwin trip in 2004.

9 August 1929 bemoaned the delay, complaining that if South Australia hadn't handed over its northern portion to the Commonwealth government, the line would have been finished much earlier. Nonetheless, the *Advertiser* hailed the railway that gave Central Australia 'communication with the sea', along with 'all the amenities of civilisation'. A 'positive El Dorado' would create new mining opportunities and enable cheaper transport of cattle and sheep in 'lands hitherto left idle'. Adelaide could now be reached in three days, instead of three weeks. In the 1950s, the Ghan, which then ran twice weekly, took more than 42 hours to traverse the 1,050-kilometre route, averaging just over 25 kilometres per hour.

The route of the original Ghan stuck close to reliable supplies of water, a prerequisite for any steam train. With the route prone to flooding, Ghan passengers could be stranded for days or even weeks en route. As with stream train travel everywhere, passengers found it hard to avoid the soot. During the Second World War, with a much-augmented service, de-mineralisation towers were built so that artesian bore water could be used, and some of the towers can still be seen. A new flood-proof route, built in the 1970s, is well to the west of the original railway line, because diesel engines don't need topping up with water. Remnants of the old Ghan rail line and its associated structures, including railway sidings, stone buildings and long-abandoned steel bridges, can still be seen by 4WD adventurers tackling the Oodnadatta Track. The Algebuckina Bridge over the Neales River is the largest of all the structures, often photographed at sunset.

The long-dreamed-of north–south continental railway reached the port of Darwin in 2003, the new track paid for by the federal, South Australian and Northern Territory governments, and private investors wishing to develop it as a major freight route. It runs through the Tanami Desert and, with permission, traverses over 1,000 kilometres of Aboriginal land. The new Ghan, a privately operated passenger train, does the trip from Adelaide to Darwin twice a week in almost the same time as the Old Ghan took to travel from Port Augusta to Alice Springs. It attracts train fans from around the world, and is particularly popular with retirees who have the time for such travel.

South Australia's century-old dream of a railway line to Darwin has finally come to fruition. In 2015, the port of Darwin was purchased by a Chinese consortium, so Adelaide now boasts a more efficient trade route to Asia than anyone envisaged in 1900.

▲ An 'Afghani Man' leads a heavily laden camel train, photographed by Frank Hurley, in 1914.

◄ The Ghan at Alice Springs in 1958.

Queensland

Carnarvon Gorge

Aboriginal Dreaming says that the rainbow serpent Mundagurra carved out the sandstone of Carnarvon Gorge as he came in and out of the river. Today, the gorge is best known for its rock art, which retains its intensity despite extreme temperatures up to the mid-40s in summer. Created using a stencilling technique and red-and-yellow ochre from the river, the art depicts hands, tools, weapons and ceremonial ornaments. After nearly 150 years of Europeans wandering about this landscape, at times degrading the art work and trespassing on sites sacred to Aboriginal people, visitors can share the experience in a respectful way with an Aboriginal ranger. Be prepared to walk.

Indigenous rock art holds a fascination for tourists, art historians and archaeologists, and has been heavily promoted for some decades. Tourists flock to see rock art at Uluru and Kakadu. Carnarvon Gorge, north of Roma, is much less accessible but still attracts thousands of visitors a year, many of them grey nomads setting up camp in the national park.

In April 1993, Jackie Huggins, her mother Rita, who had grown up in the area, and Adelaide geographer Jane Jacobs visited the gorge. In the late 1920s, a young Rita and her family were forcibly removed from their land, under the *Aborigines Protection and Restriction of Opium Act 1897*, and moved in a cattle truck to Barambah Reserve, renamed Cherbourg in 1932. Jackie, Rita and Jane wrote an article about their visit to the gorge, where they concluded that the rock art provides 'visitors with a calm and scenic experience of a pacified and naturalised Aboriginality'.

Most commentary about Indigenous rock carvings in Australia, from the early 1800s to the 1950s, begins by waxing lyrical about the ancient continent. To today's readers, some of this commentary appears patronising, but it could be respectful. In January 1936, *The Central Queensland Herald*, a Rockhampton newspaper, included the following comment in an article about Carnarvon Gorge:

In parts of this great gorge are large caves, which, years ago were used by the aboriginals for their burial grounds. Around these caves on the sandstone face of the rocks are aboriginal markings, depicting hands, feet, boomerangs, and also many other signs.

A year and a half later, amateur geographer Danny O'Brien organised a Royal Geographical Society of Queensland party of 'naturalists' to explore the gorge, catching a train to Roma, and staying overnight at a local sheep station. The four-man party had 18 saddle and pack horses for the trip. Father Leo Hayes,

◀ Rock art at Carnarvon Gorge, photographed on the 10.8-kilometre 'Art Gallery Walk' in 2013.

▲ Boolimba Bluff at sunset, looking out across the gorge.

a Catholic priest, self-trained geologist and assiduous collector of Australiana, became the spokesman for the group, and was interviewed by *The Northern Miner*, the Charters Towers newspaper:

The expedition entered the Carnarvon Gorge at an abrupt rock pinnacle called the Devil's Signboard, overlooking a deep ravine known as Hell. The party was told that no white man had ever been through this ravine. After skirting around it the travellers camped in the beginning of the Carnarvon Gorge.

'Although we were so near to Hell,' Father Hayes said, 'that day's travelling over the range was glorious. The view … with the sun shining on the sandstone walls, 1700ft to 2000ft high, was awe-inspiring. It was wild country of the

Colorado Canyon type, with open forest on the hills, and dense vegetation with beautiful timber in the gorges.'

… The expedition found many new caves in which there were fine examples of Aboriginal art. Father Hayes explained that the Aborigines anticipated modern spray painting. They took red and yellow ochre from the creek as their box of paints. They broke up the ochre, soaked it well in their mouths, placed the object they wished to depict against the cave wall, as a stencil, and blew the ochreous mixture around it. The result was a perfect outline representation. A man's own hand was the most convenient stencil. Other 'paintings' seen in the caves included boomerangs of both the returning and the fighting types, nulla nullas, stone axes complete with bark handles, dilly bags, emu feet, human feet, stone tools and implements.

By the hand prints Aboriginal artists hundreds of years ago left their signatures on their work. Father Hayes noticed that one hand mark showed the little finger cut off at the second joint. He said the native pictures in the Carnarvon caves were the best he had ever seen. It was amazing that whereas the canvas of a civilised artist would perish if exposed to the weather for centuries, these paintings on the gorge walls had remained.

Without modern radio carbon dating techniques, the men had no way of knowing the real antiquity of the paintings, but they had a sense of the significance of what they saw, and displayed genuine interest in some aspects of Indigenous culture.

Much less respectful were many trips subsequently led by Danny O'Brien for the Royal Geographical Society of Queensland. His tours were designed to promote the gorge as a tourist destination, with O'Brien taking photographs and writing promotional articles. Prospective travellers were told in one of his booklets that they could camp in an 'Aboriginal cave' but that the Aboriginal inhabitants had 'disappeared' 70 years ago. He made no mention of nineteenth-century frontier killings, nor the forced removals just 20 years earlier, nor the Indigenous community still living at nearby Springsure—other than to photograph King Chookey, and to caption him as 'the last of the tribe'. Queenslanders looking for an outback adventure camped at the park in the 1950s and home movie footage shows both men and boys placing their hands over the rock art, which had no form of protection at the time. Souveniring of Indigenous artefacts was commonplace, despite the site having been designated a national park in 1932.

When Grahame Walsh's book *The Roof of Queensland* was published in 1983, much of the rock art had already been 'shockingly disfigured', not least by successive groups of 4WD adventurers, whose main interest in the landscape and its ancient features was to crash through it. Walsh told readers of the violent clashes between 'pioneering settlers' and local tribes who fought back before being forcibly dispersed to mission stations. His book featured handsome coloured photographs of Carnarvon Gorge and its rock art.

Since then, the National Parks and Wildlife Service has gone to considerable lengths to protect the main rock art sites, sensibly not providing the public details of many of them, the best way to ensure some level of protection. There are parts of Australia now where the only way to see rock art is with an Indigenous guide, giving visitors more context and a greater sense of the meaning and the sanctity of the place.

◀ Rock art photographed by expeditioners in 1938. They thought the handprints were the work of 'Aboriginal artists hundreds of years ago'.

▼ Father Hayes' all-male expedition party photographed in 1938 enjoying a communal meal.

Cooktown

The Guugu Yimidhirr people knew that 'a mysterious white winged object passing along the surface of the ocean like a gigantic pelican' was on the way up the coastline well before Captain Cook's ship, the *Endeavour*, ran into the Great Barrier Reef in June 1770 and had to stop for repairs. Cook's crew made their first sighting of a kangaroo at Gangarr, promptly renamed Cooktown. The river where they repaired their ship was renamed Endeavour. Just over 100 years later, Cooktown became a thriving port based on the export of gold and tin. But the town economy collapsed within a few decades, many of its grand buildings and houses abandoned. With the growth of tourism to northern Queensland from the early 1970s, made possible by better road and air links, Cooktown gradually rebuilt itself, benefitting from a growing interest in both 'the Reef' and the rich Indigenous culture of the region.

Many families have pilgrimage sites, places where their forebears lived that they return to. In my family, on the paternal side, that place is Cooktown, set on the southern bank of the Endeavour River in north Queensland. Captain Cook named the river after his ship, the *Endeavour*, having spent 48 days there in 1770 to repair a hole caused by reef coral. Both my paternal grandparents were born in Cooktown in the 1890s, then a thriving settlement, which had developed rapidly from 1873 with the discovery of gold at the Palmer River, 100 kilometres inland. Thousands of miners descended on the Palmer River, most notably the Chinese, many of whom remained to start local businesses in Cooktown. Such was the optimism at the time that the *Australian Handbook* of 1876—the year the telegraph connected Brisbane to Cooktown—described the town's bright future:

> though the town has been almost born in a day, it will most likely take its place as one of the most important centres of the colony should the yield of gold continue. Already upwards of 1,000 persons are located on the spot, and the usual institutions are springing up … A recent report states that there are a great many large and handsome stores being erected, in various parts of the town, for Chinese merchants … The Australian Company's steamers ply once a fortnight, and the Torres Straits mail steamers call both going and returning

My grandfather's father was a baker and photographer, my grandmother's father a slaughterman. Leaving school at the age of 14, my grandfather worked in Spearritt's Federal Bakery, which opened in 1891. Cooktown housed a large Catholic convent and nunnery, perched up the hill from the main street, a customs house, substantial banks and numerous hotels, always a mainstay in Far North

◄ Ignaz Klauber produced this image for a Dutch audience, based on a drawing by Sydney Parkinson, the artist in Cook's party, of the Endeavour River, including Cook's 1770 campsite. Bill Gammage uses this painting in his *The Biggest Estate on Earth* (2011) as part of his evidence about the way that Indigenous people used fire to control growth, regrowth and animal populations.

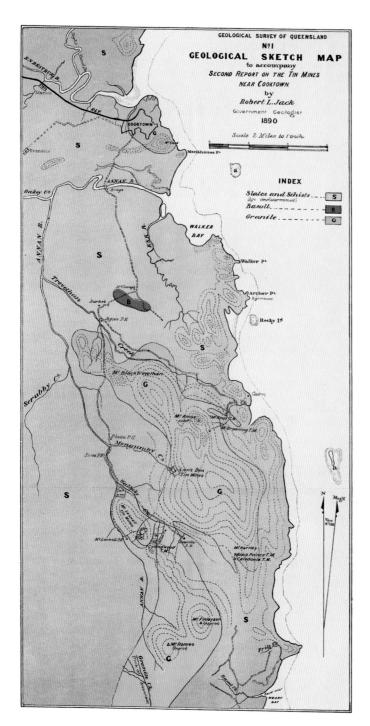

▲ Geologists assiduously surveyed Australia for mineral deposits in the later half of the nineteenth century and the early decades of the twentieth. This 1890 map shows rock types and tin deposits.

Queensland, where hot and humid conditions were and are alleviated by drinking plenty of beer. A wharf line and 50 kilometres of track from Cooktown to Normanby were in operation by 1885. Extensions to the nearby town of Laura were completed in part in the 1890s, with the opening of a five-span iron lattice girder bridge on reinforced concrete columns over the Laura River. Used only once by a test train before gold yields slumped dramatically, the whole line was declared a white elephant. Tin deposits at Annan River, south of the town, were found in 1885, making up for the declining alluvial gold yields, and shipping line and merchant company Burns Philp launched much of its New Guinea trade from Cooktown's harbour.

As the city grew, so did the residents' sense of civic pride. They set aside funds for a botanic garden, built in 1878 ❶, and for memorials to Captain Cook ❷ and Mary Watson ❸, a young wife and mother who perished in her escape from Lizard Island, where her husband had built on sacred Indigenous land. Because of Cooktown's awkward terrain, gullies were filled with locally crushed granite to create wide streets. The port extended over 2 kilometres along the river, the town hall (now the Council Chambers ❹) was spacious and the hospital ❺ had 80 beds. A school of arts housed nearly 1,900 books and a mineral and curio collection, and the Federal Hall had a skating rink.

Without further mineral discoveries, the population fell by over 50 per cent, between 1891 and 1911, with a cyclone in 1907 damaging most buildings and destroying some. Young people headed south. My grandfather, Frank, headed for Ipswich, 30 kilometres west of Brisbane, to learn the photographic trade. My grandmother, Lilas, was sent to Cairns on the death of her father in 1916, where she worked for Mrs Elliott in a boarding house.

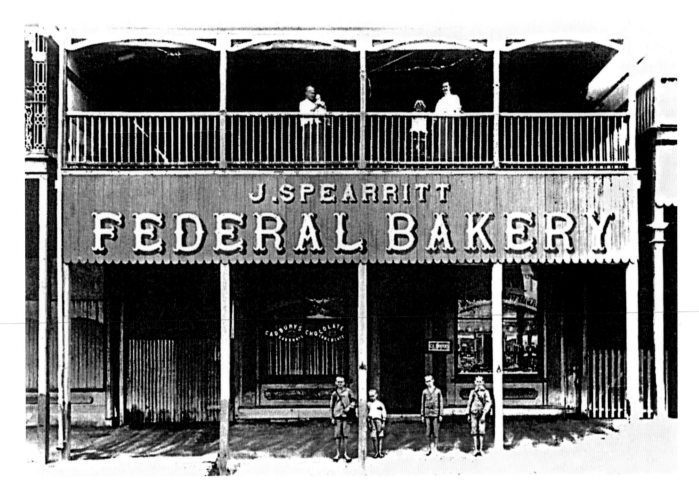

While my grandparents didn't forget Cooktown, they never went back—even though the land on which Spearritt's Federal Bakery stood remained in family hands. Everyone in north Queensland knew that Cooktown was on the skids, and it took an inordinate amount of time to get to. With only 400 people left by the time of the 1947 census, more and more buildings were abandoned. My uncle Clyde was the first family member to return in 1962, and again in 1964, when he took Frank to see what was left of the town. Cooktown was down and out.

During the Second World War, the convent and school were taken over for military purposes, which gave the town a short-lived boost. As Catholic authority had been transferred to Cairns in 1941 and the convent's sisters evacuated, the building was abandoned after the war until 1969, when tenders were called for demolition. Local pride wanted the building saved, and the Cook bicentennial year, 1970, made that possible. The convent became the James Cook Museum ⑥, operated by the National Trust of Queensland. The restoration coincided with a

▲ James and Alice Spearritt's family outside their Federal Bakery in Cooktown in 1910.

▲ Grassy Hill offers visitors a sweeping vantage point to view the Endeavour River. Charlotte Street, the main street of Cooktown, is clearly visible at left.

growing interest in far north tourism and four wheel drive adventures, and an increasing appreciation of the extensive national parks and Aboriginal cave art within the Hope Vale Aboriginal Community's land **7**. The Cooktown and District Historical Society, which specialises in local genealogy, occupies the Queensland National Bank Building **8**, as a museum for Cooktown history. Its displays include needlework by my great aunt.

I had my first visit to Cooktown in 1980, when it took us six hours to drive from Cairns on a very rough gravel road. On this family holiday, my father didn't want to sign on for a rental car, because the agreement specifically stated that you were not allowed to drive the car to Cooktown. So instead, with limited assets, I signed the rental agreement for a family trip. The view of the Endeavour River, from Grassy Hill **9** above the town, is breathtaking. We wandered about the abandoned site of Spearritt's Federal Bakery **10**, excited to find remnant bottles in the decayed foundations.

Today, visitors get to Cooktown on a cruise ship, fly or drive on a sealed road from Cairns in three hours. Charlotte Street, the commanding thoroughfare abutting the Endeavour River, often throngs with backpackers, grey nomads and cruise ship

day-trippers. By the 2016 census, Cooktown's population had risen to 2,631, almost a return to its 1890s figure. Travellers interested in Indigenous heritage can visit the Hope Vale Aboriginal Community.

Explore the history

1 COOKTOWN BOTANIC GARDENS
Walker St, Finch Bay

2 CAPTAIN COOK MONUMENT
Esplanade, Bicentennial Park

3 MARY WATSON FOUNTAIN
Charlotte St

4 COOK SHIRE COUNCIL CHAMBERS
Charlotte St

5 OLD COOKTOWN HOSPITAL
May St

6 JAMES COOK HISTORICAL MUSEUM
Furneaux St

7 HOPE VALE COMMUNITY
Hope Vale

8 QUEENSLAND NATIONAL BANK BUILDING
Charlotte St

9 GRASSY HILL LOOKOUT
Hope St

10 SPEARRITT'S FEDERAL BAKERY SITE
112 Charlotte St

Great Barrier Reef

Stretching more than 2,300 kilometres along the Queensland coast and comprising almost 3,000 individual reefs, the Great Barrier Reef has been listed as a World Heritage Site for nearly 40 years. The current reefs are over 6,000 years old and are home to a diverse array of marine animals and plants, from 1,600 types of fish to molluscs, sharks, corals and 500 species of worm. The Great Barrier Reef is a refuge for turtles to lay their eggs, including six of the world's seven marine turtle species. In 2014, then US president Barack Obama expressed concern about the health of the reef, saying he wanted his daughters' children to be able to visit. Threats to this world wonder—from climate change and tourism to a massive expansion of Queensland's export coal ports—remain a matter of international concern.

Most visitors to the Great Barrier Reef see it first from the air, flying to Cairns or Townsville or one of the island resorts with its own airstrip. It is a stupendous sight, the world's largest coral reef system. Captain Cook encountered the reef when the *Endeavour* ran into it on 11 June 1770, off the coast of a place he promptly named Cooktown. Cook had avoided running into the reef before by sailing relatively close to shore. Two hundred and forty years later, the *Shen Neng 1* coal carrier, en route from the port of Gladstone to China, ran aground on the Douglas Shoal, 70 kilometres east of Great Keppel Island. The 65,000-tonne laden vessel gouged into the reef for three kilometres. Fearing that the ship might break up, the crew could not return it to Gladstone, but some of the cargo was unloaded in Hervey Bay before it proceeded north.

Naturalists and later conservationists have advocated for the protection of the reef for well over a century. Before the 1970s, most concerns revolved around protecting species and habitats, especially the survival of dugongs and turtles, endangered by hunting and net fishing. With the completion of the coastal railway to Cairns in 1924 and the growing popularity of north Queensland with southerners escaping their winter, the Queensland government took a modest interest in preserving some aspects of the local environment. Green Island, popular as a day-trip destination from Cairns, was proclaimed a national park in 1937; Heron Island, east of Gladstone, became a national park in 1943, with flying boats delivering holiday-makers after the Second World War. Whitsunday Island followed in 1944, preventing further timber clearing.

Green Island offered an underwater observatory, the Coral Cay Hotel, and in the late 1960s catered for 'the experienced traveller—the people with money who resent the overcrowded cities'. Marketing for north Queensland has long focused on southerners, those 'unfortunate servants of commerce' who 'brave the elements and arrive at work chilled by angry winter'. As late as 1970, a tourist booklet

◄ The interplay of coral and water produces magnificent hues, captured here by photographer Richard Woldendorp in 1996.

published by a leading Cairns photographer, explained that 'beachcoming life is very infectious and you may find yourself with a new philosophy of living, and an urge to find and buy your own island'. The same booklet included an article on how to keep Great Barrier Reef fish in your home aquarium.

A concerted campaign by conservationists, including the poet Judith Wright, and a considerable body of marine scientists, persuaded the federal government to create the Great Barrier Reef Marine Park in 1975, against the strong objections of the Bjelke-Petersen government in Queensland, which retained fond hopes of being able to mine the reef for oil. Fortunately, none was ever found.

Listed as a World Heritage Area in 1981, the Great Barrier Reef now faces severe challenges from infestations, the crown-of-thorns starfish being the most notable example, port dredging, run-off from agricultural land on the mainland, damage from coal ships and climate change, especially increasing water temperatures and rising sea levels.

Tourism operators, who once had a rather cavalier approach to the environment, are now among the loudest voices in trying to protect the reef. Reef travel companies know that their business will simply fade away if the reef suffers more damage. Mining companies on the other hand continue to lobby for ever larger port facilities, demanding dredging for the giant coal ships en route to India, China and elsewhere in Asia.

The writer E.J. Banfield brought the Great Barrier Reef to the attention of the world. Liverpool-born, he moved from Victoria to North Queensland in the 1880s and worked on *The Townsville Daily Bulletin*. Diagnosed as tubercular, he settled with his wife on Dunk Island in 1897, surviving on locally grown food, fish and supplies from the weekly steamer that plied the islands. Considering his island a natural sanctuary, Banfield produced a tourist guide to North Queensland, *Within the Barrier* (1907). His first major book, *The Confessions of a Beachcomber*, originally published in London in 1908, became an international bestseller. He died on the island in 1923. After his wife died ten years later, the island became a tourist resort, and now houses 400 guests.

While many of the reef islands remain uninhabited, others have a complex and troubled history. Declared an Aboriginal Reserve by the Queensland government in 1914, Palm Island's population grew rapidly from 1918, when a cyclone destroyed the settlement on the Hull River. In 1938, the writer Clem Christesen reported 'a uniform system of village streets beautified with avenues of coconut palms and mango trees'. The village houses were mainly of plaited coconut leaves or thatch, with many islanders owning their own poultry runs and piggeries. Some got work on the cattle stations and sugar plantations on the mainland while others fished for pearl shell. For the winter cruise season, 'the natives provide spectacular corroborees and interesting displays of dancing and action songs'. A tourist in

▲ The Barrier Reef and its many islands have been actively marketed since the 1920s. By the time this brochure was produced in the 1960s, most southerners arrived by plane, as the train trip from Sydney or Melbourne took many days.

▶ When James Northfield created this poster in 1932, most visitors to the reef came by boat or train.

search of further adventure could go turtle riding (very popular with ladies), deep sea fishing, 'bombing' for reef fish or return to the mainland to shoot crocodiles. Palm Island made headlines in November 2004. Sergeant Chris Hurley had arrested Cameron Doomadgee for swearing. Forty minutes later, Doomadgee was found dead in his cell from internal injuries. A riot broke out and the police station was burnt down. A coronial inquest found that the sergeant lost his temper and fatally assaulted Doomadgee. Hurley was acquitted of a manslaughter charge, and a further coronial inquest found that the injuries were not 'intentionally inflicted'.

The Great Barrier Reef Marine Park Authority administers 345,000 square kilometres of marine park, which, at its widest point, extends 400 kilometres east of Mackay. It includes 3,000 unconnected coral reefs and 300 reef islands or sand cays, one third of which are vegetated. Today's reefs are about 8,500 years old, sitting above layers of reef and alluvium dating back at least two million years. The reef has 1,625 types of fish and 600 types of hard and soft corals.

As Australia's greatest natural tourist attraction, the reef is subject to two very different development pressures: tourist development and coal loading facilities, both of which the Authority has to try to prevent or at least temper. In the 1990s, half of Bright Point on Magnetic Island was removed, the excavated rock used to create a new, all-weather ferry and boat harbour, with steel beams inserted into the coral beds below.

Both the reef and the islands are often damaged by cyclones, the most recent being Cyclone Yasi in 2011, with Hinchinbrook Island in the eye of the storm, and the category 5 Cyclone Marcia in 2015. An overdeveloped marina facility at Cardwell saw massive damage. Today we know from extensive scientific evidence that the greatest threat the reef faces is from global warming, as its marine diversity depends on water temperature at around 20 degrees.

◄ A popular tourist pastime for some decades, riding on the back of a turtle is no longer considered an environmentally friendly activity. When Frank Hurley took this photograph in 1962, such concerns were still some years away.

▶ This photograph of Palm Island, taken in 1946 by Jack Band, depicts a serene place. However, the forceful removal of Indigenous people from various parts of Queensland to Palm Island was far from serene.

Ipswich Railway Workshops

Railways opened up the state of Queensland for people and goods and led to the development of local industries to manufacture locomotives, rolling stock and all the myriad parts required to keep a railway going. A model layout of the vast state railway network, on display at the Ipswich Railway Workshops Museum, testifies to the importance of the railways. See and hear functioning locomotives, carriages from a more luxurious era of train travel and the bustle of a platform at departure time. Equally popular with children and adults, the Workshops Museum brings back the great age of steam, and explains why railways continue to be vital to Australia, not least in moving heavy freight for export.

From the construction of the first railways in the 1850s until the coming of mass car ownership in the 1960s, most longer journeys in Australia were by train. The first railway line in Queensland, from Ipswich to Toowoomba, was built between 1865 and 1867 to transport wool from the Darling Downs, while freight to Brisbane went by the river. The rail link to Brisbane did not open until 1875, by which time the Ipswich Railway Workshops had been operating for 11 years. The Ipswich mines produced three-quarters of Queensland's coal, so the rail lines were kept busy. Coastal shipping remained important for distant ports, including Townsville, Darwin and Broome, but railways linked all but one of the mainland capital cities to each other by the late nineteenth century, finally getting to Perth when the 'Trans-Australian Railway' crossed the continent in 1917.

While most locomotives and rolling stock were initially imported from Britain, they still had to be adapted to Australian circumstances. Railway gangs throughout the continent were hard at work laying new track and building culverts and bridges. In the latter decades of the nineteenth century, the major rail lines went outwards from the capital cities, including Sydney, Melbourne, Adelaide, Hobart and Perth. The exception was Queensland, where the state was so large and the demand for rail freight so extensive that four separate railway systems went east to west, from the major ports of Brisbane, Rockhampton, Townsville and Cairns to their respective hinterlands. The coastal railway line from Brisbane to Cairns was not completed until 1924. At its height, in 1932, the Queensland railways had 10,500 kilometres of working track, more than any other state. From the 1960s to the 1990s, many spur lines, once used to carry dairy produce, cattle and wheat, were closed, while new lines were established to bring coal and iron intended for export from open cut mines to the ports. Even today, Queensland has over 8,000 kilometres of working rail lines.

In the twentieth century, the Ipswich Railway Workshops built locomotives, freight and passenger carriages. Each workshop on site had its own culture, from carpentry to the metal foundry, and workers were not allowed into neighbouring

◄ The Ipswich Railway Workshops Museum captures the rich history of the railway workshops, which once employed thousands of workers.

Carriage Shop, Ipswich Railway Works.

Sangster Monument, North Ipswich.

Tower House and Pattern Shop, Ipswich Railway.

Greetings from Ipswich

Carriage Shop, Ipswich Workshop.

Band Rotunda, North Ipswich.

Erecting Shop, Ipswich Railway Works.

▲ The size and complexity of the workshops is well captured in this c.1910 postcard.

▶ This 1939 railway map of Queensland shows the vast extent of the railway system, including the east–west routes, from Brisbane to Charleville, from Rockhampton to Longreach and Winton, and from Townsville to Charters Towers, Hughenden and Cloncurry, with terminating branch lines beyond all those places.

▼ Workers at the Ipswich Railway Workshops in 1913, proud of their trades.

workshops. It was a proud, skilled, highly unionised, blue-collar culture. Employment peaked during both world wars, when the workshops produced munitions and catered for other wartime demands. The workshops went into decline in the 1950s, with new diesel trains being sent to other locations for maintenance. The workshops just managed to hang on when the employment base of the surrounding city, including mines and industry, went into rapid decline, surviving on the site long enough to attract a heritage listing and the support of the state government as a campus of the Queensland Museum.

One of the great attractions of the workshops, now open to the public, is that much of the remaining equipment still works, which marks these workshops out from equivalents elsewhere in Australia, including Eveleigh in Sydney and Newport in Melbourne, where buildings have been gutted and re-used, reflecting much higher property values. Not everyone enjoys admiring old locomotives, but few can resist the temptation to wander along the corridor of a 1920s carriage, with its magnificent wooden lining, metal ceilings and framed black and white photographs of tourist scenes. For the mechanically minded, the huge traverser can still move locomotives and carriages from one shed to another, a sight to behold. There is no better place in Australia to get a sense of the great age of rail.

If a prime minister was 'egged' today, it's hard to imagine that the perpetrator wouldn't be arrested immediately. But that didn't happen in November 1917 at Warwick Railway Station, 130 kilometres south-west of Brisbane, when a well-aimed egg knocked off Prime Minister Billy Hughes' hat. A wartime leader who left the Labor Party to lead a conservative government, Hughes campaigned vigorously in favour of conscription for overseas service. He was so cross at the failure of the Irish-dominated Queensland police force to arrest the culprit, that as soon as his train got to Sydney he issued orders to establish a federal police force.

Conscription for overseas service proved to be the most divisive issue in Australia during the First World War. Prime Minister Billy Hughes, a short, fiery Welshman, and former trade union leader, was expelled by the Labor Party for his support of conscription, and with 23 Labor supporters he joined the conservatives and retained the prime ministership. Having lost the first conscription referendum, Hughes threw himself into the second, in December 1917, with gusto. Rotten eggs and unripe fruit were common missiles used by his assailants at increasingly rowdy public meetings, and Hughes took to carrying a pistol.

The Queensland Labor Premier, T.J. Ryan, a trade unionist and Irishman, despised turncoats like Hughes. Ryan saw the Great War as yet another example of British imperialism, and became Hughes' most vocal opponent. Ryan told the Queensland parliament that the 'conscriptionists' wanted to hand the 'young democracy of Australia' to 'capitalists' and 'exploiters'. He attacked the Commonwealth government's War Precautions Act as an attempt to 'destroy unionism' and to impose censorship. Hughes himself, often known for rash acts, took part in a raid on the Queensland government printing office in what proved a fruitless attempt to grab all copies of Ryan's speech.

Two days later, on 29 November, Hughes set out for Sydney, to address pro-conscription rallies in Toowoomba and Warwick. When his train drew in at the elegant sandstone Warwick Railway Station, his supporters accompanied him to the platform. Sergeant Kenny, the senior Queensland police officer present, was standing by Hughes as he addressed the crowd, when an egg struck the Prime Minister's hat, and another broke in front of him. Hughes demanded the arrest of the culprits, Irish-born brothers Bart and Pat Brosnan, and jumped down into the crowd when Pat gave him the finger. Luckily for the brothers, who were well-known to local police, Hughes had left his pistol on the train. The men were removed from the platform, with Bart bleeding heavily, having been punched in the face by Hughes supporters. After a night in the lockup, Pat Brosnan was released with a ten shilling fine for creating a disturbance.

◀ Jim Case, cartoonist for the union-owned *Worker* newspaper in Brisbane, relished giving Billy Hughes a 'no majority' egg in the eye. Hughes had just lost his second conscription referendum in December 1917.

◄ In the euphoria at the end of the Great War, 'the war to end all wars', Prime Minister Hughes is carried aloft by troops returning from the front. Of the almost 420,000 who enlisted, more than 60,000 lost their lives.

Read
"The Australian Worker"

CONSCRIPTION
MEANS SLAVERY

VOTE NO

Issued by W. H. LAMBERT,
Central Branch, A.W.U.

Vote
YES
For Reinforcements.
Help the Boys at the Front!

Queen City
Printers
Pty. Ltd.

▲ The language of the 'yes' and 'no' campaigns is well captured in these badges.

The Warwick Egg Incident took just 13 minutes, after which Hughes resumed his train journey to Sydney. At Wallangarra, he sent a telegram to the Queensland Commissioner of Police, stating that Sergeant Kenny had refused to arrest the 'two prominent ringleaders' for 'a deliberate and violent breach' of Commonwealth law. Kenny told Hughes that 'he recognised the laws of Queensland only'. At subsequent rallies in New South Wales, Hughes embellished the Warwick Egg Incident, using it as evidence of the lengths to which supporters of Queensland Premier Ryan would go—even though eggs were often thrown at public meetings by both pro- and anti-conscriptionists. An official Queensland Police inquiry found that, apart from the egg, there had been no assault on Hughes. Hughes' biographer, L.F. Fitzhardinge, concluded that Hughes was 'well over the edge of hysteria, losing control of himself'.

On his return to Sydney, a furious Hughes portrayed both Premier Ryan and the Queensland Police Force as Sinn Feiners (the group opposed to the British rule of Ireland) and radical trade unionists, and promptly established a Commonwealth Police Force to offer personal protection to the prime minister and other ministers, and to protect federal property and ports, where left-wing wharfies were a powerful force.

Hughes lost the second conscription referendum just a fortnight later. The 'no' majority had grown from 72,476 to 166,588 votes and only two states voted in favour, Western Australia and Tasmania, along with the federal territories.

The Warwick Egg Incident, well-known in Queensland, is almost unheard of anywhere else in the nation. The incident is re-enacted on special occasions, with relatives of the Brosnan brothers in attendance. For many, it remains an amusing parable of a proud Queensland country town not succumbing to prime ministerial bullying. It is also a reminder of an era when public meetings mattered, and politicians had to face the electorate, rather than hiding behind minders and security officers. While the railway station now only services freight, not passengers, one can still visit the site of this notable event in Australian history, the catalyst for the creation of what is now called the Australian Federal Police.

▲ Warwick Railway Station
in 1911, a centre for both
freight and passenger
transport.

◄ The station, photographed
here in 2009, is today
the scene of regular
re-enactments of the
Warwick Egg Incident.

South Australia

Burra

Burra and its copper mines were central to the progress of a struggling South Australia in the mid-nineteenth century. As mining in Cornwall declined, its copper miners looked to Britain's imperial colonies for new prospects, but copper is quickly mined out. Burra's miners headed for the goldfields of the eastern states. A rich array of heritage structures, the location for the making of the film *Breaker Morant* and an internationally recognised heritage conservation agreement (the Burra Charter) make Burra well worth a visit.

The remains of Cornish copper mines ❶ ❷ ❸ above the town of Burra in South Australia present a stark landscape. Remnant industrial structures of brick and stone dot the bare red hills. Visitors wander around the site of what was once a place of frenzied mining and smelting. Two hours' drive north of Adelaide, and only half an hour from the vineyards of the Clare Valley, the charming town is popular with both day and weekend tourists.

Australia has many notable mining sites. But Burra has an international significance well beyond its historical importance as a copper mine. In 1979, members of Australia ICOMOS (International Council on Monuments and Sites) met in Burra to debate a charter of heritage conservation suitable for Australian circumstances. Unlike the world's first main heritage document—the Venice Charter, developed in 1964—the Australian meeting did not recommend conserving or altering structures to take them back to an imagined primary point of heritage significance. Rather the gathering concluded that heritage conservation should take into account successive uses of a place or structure. When an addition or renovation is needed for practical purposes, the charter recommends the use of a different material, for instance steel with a stone building, so visitors can appreciate that they are looking at a modern alteration, not a pretend heritage extension. The Burra Charter has had worldwide influence on how buildings and places are conserved. Examples of this approach can be seen at the Brisbane Customs House and at the Museum of Modern Art in Sydney (housed in the former headquarters of the Maritime Services Board), where the additions are distinct from the original structures.

Copper was first discovered in Australia in Kapunda, 70 kilometres north of Adelaide, in 1842, and mines and a township soon grew up. Two shepherds discovered the Burra deposits in 1845 and mining leases followed. By 1848, the mines employed 567 men and the following year smelting began, using coal imported from Newcastle. The township had a Wesleyan Chapel ❹, two hotels ❺, a brewery ❻ and a privately run school ❼. Catholic ❽ and Anglican ❾ churches were erected in the same period, some of which have survived to this day.

◀ Morphett's Enginehouse Museum, with the open cut mine in the foreground, in 2014.

▲ Samuel Thomas Gill's 1848 painting of Kooringa, the Burra township. Bush vegetation has made way for cattle, while a dispossessed Aboriginal family group is portrayed surveying an altered landscape.

The copper mine proved very lucrative, growing to a population of over 1,000 workers by 1851. But the following year most miners abandoned Burra and set out for the Victorian goldfields. The mines gradually returned to production in the latter half of the 1850s, with the addition of a candle factory to supply light below ground. The town's population had ballooned to over 4,000, warranting a gaol ⑩, a courthouse ⑪, a National Bank ⑫ and a cricket club. The telegraph ⑬ was installed by 1860.

By 1865, the mine was losing money, and the price of copper had fallen from 110 pounds per ton to 8 pounds per ton. As the mines got deeper, the cost of extraction increased, so the owners turned to open cut mining, the first to do so in

Australia. Despite the success of the open-cut technique in separating out the ore, the Burra operation could no longer pay its way, as the best ore bodies petered out. In September 1877, the mine closed after 32 years, with the remaining 300 workers losing their jobs.

The arrival of the railway in 1870 had made wheat transport possible and this partly offset the declining fortunes of the mine. The denuded landscape, exacerbated by a rabbit plague in the mid-1870s, gave the brand new newspaper and its readers plenty to comment on, as did a 20-foot landslide at nearby Spring Bank, when most of a train fell into a small ravine, killing three railway workers.

▶ These railway tracks have lain idle for 20 years, but the station retains its charm and its memories in this sunrise photo by Stephen Warren, taken in 2016. The water tower, vital for steam trains, is located just beyond the end of the platform, while a ghostly wheat silo still stands in the distance.

By the mid-1880s, the town's population stood at 2,500, half its peak. Unemployed miners left the area, many heading for Broken Hill, which by 1888 was accessible by rail. Another rabbit plague in 1904 saw well over 16,000 rabbits destroyed in just a few weeks. Mouse plagues were also common, further reinforcing the denuded mining landscape. The township itself became a civilised oasis, surrounded by abandoned mines. An elegant King's Memorial Rotunda **14**, to Edward VII, opened in 1911, in a green, well-watered civic landscape.

Like cities and towns throughout Australia, the residents of Burra suffered from the worldwide influenza epidemic in 1919. Residents seeking relief could go to Semaphore, one of the Adelaide beaches readily accessible by train. In 1922, Prime Minister Billy Hughes unveiled the Burra and District Fallen Soldier's Memorial **15** in Market Square. The same year, anthropologists identified a major Aboriginal encampment, with many artefacts surviving.

A number of attempts to re-open the mine failed, not least because of the fluctuating, and usually low, price of copper. The township declined rapidly, houses were moved elsewhere and in 1921 the chimney stack for Morphett's Enginehouse **16** was blown up for building stone. The house itself burned down in 1925, the fire started by young boys smoking out rabbits. In 1932, at the height of the Great Depression, Sir Charles Kingsford Smith landed at Burra in the *Southern Cross* and those locals who could afford it paid for a ride. By then the town's population was static. After the war, successive South Australian and Commonwealth governments were the major sources of funding for new structures, from wheat silos abutting the railway line, to a new post office and a swimming pool in 1960, when the road to Adelaide finally became bitumen all the way.

The district council acquired the Burra mine area in 1961, and officially marketed it as a tourist site. The National Trust opened a local museum five years later. The film *Breaker Morant* was made in and around Burra in 1979, a Tourist Information Office opening the same year. By 1986, passenger rail services had ceased, while grain trains last used the line in 1998–1999. The delightful 1883 station **17** fell into disrepair, but enthusiastic locals lobbied the state government to fund a full restoration, and since 2015 the station has again been open to the public, but not the railway line.

Explore
the history

1 **HISTORIC BURRA MINE SITE**

2 **BON ACCORD MINE COMPLEX**
Cnr West St and Railway Tce

3 **BURRA MINERS' DUGOUTS**
Access via Market St

4 **BURRA UNITING CHURCH
(SITE OF FIRST WESLEYAN CHAPEL)**
Cnr Chapel and Bath Sts

5 **BURRA HOTEL (FORMER MINERS
ARMS HOTEL)**
Market Sq

6 **UNICORN BREWERY CELLARS**
Bridge Tce

7 **BURRA COMMUNITY SCHOOL
(FORMER MODEL SCHOOL)**
Smelts Rd

8 **ST JOSEPH'S CATHOLIC CHURCH**
Market St

9 **ST MARY'S ANGLICAN CHURCH**
Market St

10 **REDRUTH GAOL**
Tregony St, North Burra

11 **REDRUTH COURTHOUSE**
Sancreed St, North Burra

12 **NATIONAL BANK BUILDING**
Market St

13 **FORMER TELGRAPH STATION
AND POST OFFICE**
Market St

14 **KING'S MEMORIAL ROTUNDA**
Market Sq

15 **BURRA AND DISTRICT FALLEN
SOLDIER'S MEMORIAL**
Market Sq

16 **MORPHETT'S ENGINEHOUSE
MUSEUM**
Burra Mine Site

17 **BURRA RAILWAY STATION**
Railway Tce, North Burra

Seppeltsfield Winery
and Mausoleum

From the political and economic turbulence of mid-nineteenth-century Europe to the New-World colony of South Australia, tenacious Prussians worked hard to establish Australia's oldest winery. It remains one of the country's major wine producers but, like most large vineyards, is now in corporate rather than family hands. The best place to get a sense of the scale of what is both a winery and a township is to walk up the hill to the Seppeltsfield Mausoleum, containing the remains of 28 family members. At the cellars below, you can even sample Tawny from your own birth-year.

Approaching Seppeltsfield winery in the Barossa Valley is an extraordinary experience. Suddenly, a vast array of stone and masonry structures greets you, along with a huge Grecian-style family mausoleum, built in 1927. You are led to it up a grand avenue of date palms, planted during the Great Depression.

Australia has a number of historic vineyards, dating back to the nineteenth century. Of surviving vineyards, the Jesuits' Sevenhill, established in 1851 in the Clare Valley of South Australia, and Chateau Tahbilk, established ten years later in the Nagambie Lakes of Central Victoria, are notable. But none is grander than Seppeltsfield, once a township in its own right.

Joseph Ernst Seppelt left his tobacco and liqueur factory in Prussia in 1849, at a time of great upheaval in Europe, with his wife, children, factory workers and 13 other families. Settling in South Australia, he first tried growing tobacco, without success, before purchasing land in the Barossa Valley in 1851. Wheat proved a remunerative crop because of demand from the goldfields. Seppelt also began to grow grapes, reflecting his European training and business experience. The second generation of Seppelts, Benno and his wife Sophie Schroeder, had 16 children, 13 of whom survived into adulthood. Although Benno lacked the European education of his father, he did learn agricultural chemistry from the Tanunda Vintners and Gardeners Association, which drew on the strong German community in the area. Successive generations of Seppelts developed the site, and by the late nineteenth century they were employing up to 100 workers. Later Seppelts studied at Roseworthy Agricultural College and the Royal Viticultural Institute in Vienna. The family took the horticultural aspects of vineyards and the chemistry of production very seriously.

By the start of the twentieth century, Seppelts was Australia's largest winery, producing over two million litres each year. Such was the extent of the enterprise, that apart from their own 600 hectares they also purchased grapes from nearby growers. Like the vineyards in Rutherglen, Victoria, Seppelts concentrated on fortified wines, especially port and claret, winning prizes in Sydney and overseas. In 1916, Seppelts purchased Chateau Tanunda from the Adelaide Wine Company,

◀ Seppelts, vignerons and distillers, published this price list in 1900.

▶ The photographer Wolfgang Sievers captured the winery in 1959, with the workers in gumboots on a slippery floor.

▼ The Seppelt family mausoleum, built in 1927, has a commanding site, with its avenue of date palms.

which Camillo Seppelt managed until his death in 1935. Two thousand people attended his funeral, demonstrating the affection that the Barossa Valley held for the family, and like other Seppelts he is interred in the family mausoleum.

Continuing to expand, the family purchased the Great Western vineyards in 1918, which gave them a firm base in the sparkling wine business. Becoming a publicly listed company in 1970, Seppelts was taken over by SA Brewing in 1984, and by Penfolds in 1991, under the corporate umbrella of Southcorp Wines.

If you want to get a sense of the historic landscape of an Australian vineyard—before vineyards became the targets for corporate agglomeration—there is no better place to visit than Seppeltsfield. Here you sense a rich history of European winemaking, in a village setting of great charm. Even if you can't afford the Para Liqueur Port, first laid down in barrels in 1878, you can still enjoy the ambience of one of our most historic vineyards.

◀ This Sievers' 1959 photograph reveals the enormous size of the vineyard, with castellated towers and large, elegant industrial structures in the middle ground, including the distillery. At that time, many processes in the vineyard were still very labour intensive, including hand-labelling of bottles.

Tasmania

Port Arthur

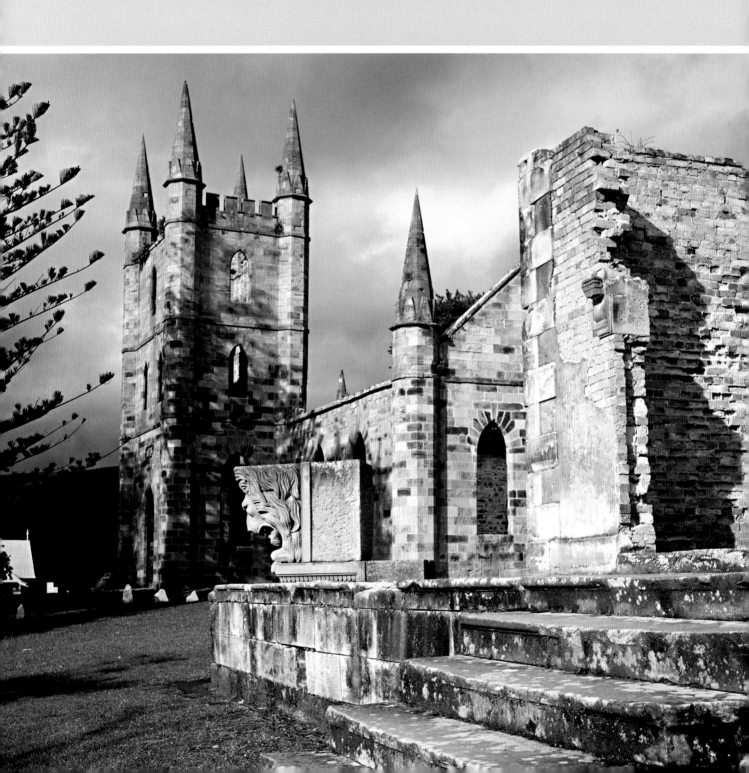

Australia's best-known convict site only served as a prison for 44 years. Soon after it closed, Port Arthur became a tourist destination and is now a World Heritage Site. More than a century after the brutal colonial penal system ended, a modern-day horror was inflicted here at the hands of a lone gunman in Australia's deadliest mass shooting. The violent history of the site, and the remarkable beauty of its buildings and setting, have inspired authors and filmmakers—and prompted strong political action to strengthen Australia's gun laws.

Port Arthur is Australia's largest and most elaborate penal settlement. From 1830, convicts cleared bush, sawed timber, made bricks and hewed stone. By the 1840s, over 1,100 convicts were at the site, with some substantial buildings reflecting their hard labour, all set in what today is regarded as a picturesque coastal landscape, rather than an isolated prison. Draconian living conditions, including poor diet and freezing winters, meant that many convicts, if not pardoned, did not live long. Convicts engaged in timber-getting were usually in leg irons, while those undertaking gardening jobs had greater freedom, as did any who displayed a talent for carpentry or building work. A flour mill and granary, erected in 1842, became the basis for a grand penitentiary building in 1857, able to accommodate 480 convicts. Today, this is Port Arthur's most imposing ruin, not least because it was gutted by fire in 1897, losing its roof.

Britain had been sending convicts to Australia since 1788, when the first fleet occupied Sydney Cove. Most convicts had committed relatively minor offences, but some of those who re-offended on arrival were sent to Port Arthur. Many of the convicts were relatively young adults, from city slums or poor rural areas. One in five were women, sometimes accompanied by a child.

Timber-getting became the main source of commercial income for Port Arthur by 1850, when a steam-powered sawmill was installed. Timber from Port Arthur and other penal sites, including Cascades, helped recoup some running costs, until the nearby slopes had been almost completely denuded. Tramways and log slides were used to get timber to waiting ships.

Port Arthur captured the imagination of novelists with its ready-made true stories of suffering and as a setting for invented plots. Nineteenth-century guides included concocted tales of escaping convicts eaten by sharks. Marcus Clarke, in his epic novel *For the Term of His Natural Life* (1874), made up a story of two boy convicts entering into a suicide pact. The novel was the basis of many adaptations including a silent film in 1927, a radio serial in 1940 and a TV miniseries in 1983.

▼ In 1827, 15-year-old John Moran, a factory boy from Lancashire, was sentenced to seven years' transportation for stealing shoes. An habitual re-offender, he spent 14 years on Norfolk Island, with a short stint in Van Diemen's Land. Sent to Port Arthur in 1855 for passing forged cheques, he gained his ticket of leave in 1874, about the time this portrait was taken.

◄ When Peter Dombrovskis took this photograph in 1973, Port Arthur got fewer than 50,000 visitors a year. Today it receives well over 300,000 visitors per annum.

◀ The Port Arthur penitentiary, depicted in a French publication in 1854, located in 'Terre de Van-Diemen'.

▼ This poster, from the late 1940s, depicts a serene Port Arthur, where the ruins of the convict church and the manicured gardens are reminiscent of a European landscape, replete with a tranquil lake. In fact, the waters around Port Arthur can be rough.

Port Arthur closed as a penal settlement in 1877 and was given over to a variety of private interests. Renamed 'Carnarvon' to remove the convict stain, much of the site was sold for residences and a new settlement grew up amid the ruins. Cricket and lawn tennis were available to both residents and the growing number of curious visitors. In a society that didn't think it had anything much 'historic'—unlike the grand cathedrals of Europe for example—picturesque convict ruins had a very particular appeal. Bushfires in the 1890s added to the sense of ruin.

A Scenery Preservation Board, created by the Tasmanian government in 1916, sought to cope with increasing numbers of tourists, who were then accommodated in hotels and guest houses on the site, re-using convict structures. Many visitors came by boat from Hobart. The 'Port Arthur' nomenclature was reinstated in 1927, not least because it capitalised on the site's convict notoriety. Management of Port Arthur came under the National Parks and Wildlife Service in the 1970s, and in 1987 a Management Authority was created. In 2010, Port Arthur became one of 11 Australian convict sites to gain World Heritage listing, along with Norfolk Island and Cockatoo Island.

Port Arthur's symbolic resonance as Australia's primary convict penal site received a grim boost in 1996. On Sunday 28 April 1996, a young man from Hobart, Martin Bryant, went on a shooting rampage, killing two people he knew near the Port Arthur site. He then entered the site, ate a meal at the Broad Arrow Cafe, opened a large bag and began shooting lunchtime visitors with an automatic rifle, killing 20 men, women and children in 90 seconds. His rampage continued in and beyond the site, ending when he killed a hostage in a nearby farmhouse, which he then set on fire. Forced out by the flames, the police captured him alive. He was charged with 35 murders and sentenced to life imprisonment without parole. Reports of the massacre made front page headlines throughout the world. All Australian states and the federal government introduced stringent controls on the sale of automatic weapons, which remain among the strictest in the world. Although lone shooter massacres have occurred in many countries over the past few decades, the 'Port Arthur Massacre' has the dubious distinction of having the largest death toll inflicted by a single individual on Australian soil.

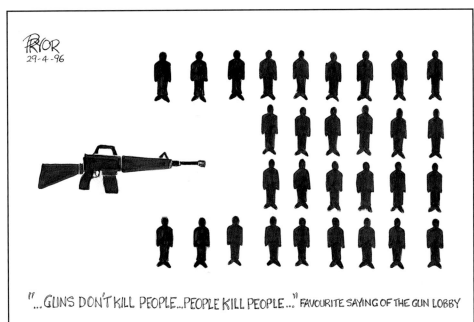

"...GUNS DON'T KILL PEOPLE...PEOPLE KILL PEOPLE..." FAVOURITE SAYING OF THE GUN LOBBY

▲ A panorama of Port Arthur in 2013.

◀ The day after the Port Arthur massacre, *Canberra Times* cartoonist Geoff Pryor drew this memorable image, questioning the logic of gun lobby propaganda. Prime Minister John Howard successfully pushed for strict gun laws and an amnesty for the public to hand over unlicensed weapons.

Save the Franklin

The fight to save the Franklin River from damming is a classic example of the struggle between those determined to harness nature to promote development and those who see its preservation as a moral responsibility. This was not just a Tasmanian or an Australian battle; world attention centred on the majestic Franklin River, with international celebrities supporting the conservation cause. Protesters blockaded the proposed dam site and machinery, resulting in arrests that put pressure on Tasmania's prisons. Songs written for the cause became bestsellers and a photograph by Peter Dombrovskis of Rock Island Bend has become one of the most famous in Australian history. A triumph for the power of non-violent protest, the success of the 'Save the Franklin' campaign has inspired conservationists ever since.

Having failed to save Lake Pedder from flooding by the Hydro-Electric Commission (HEC) in the early 1970s, passionate Tasmanian environmentalists formed their own Wilderness Society, led by local GP Bob Brown. In 1981, Indigenous cave sites of great antiquity were discovered on the lower Franklin and the federal government nominated Tasmania's south-west for World Heritage status.

The genesis of this battle can be traced to the late nineteenth century, when electrification and a clean and reliable water supply were the two great signs of modernity. Most Australian power stations were powered by coal, and many cities, including Brisbane, Sydney and Melbourne, had nearby coal supplies. The power stations were restricted to where the consumers were, usually near city centres, except in Victoria where brown coal-fired stations were located in the Yallourn Valley.

Tasmania didn't have sufficient coal supplies to manufacture electricity but it did have some high-rainfall, mountainous landscapes. Hydroelectric power plants, running off dammed water and the energy this generated, seemed the obvious answer. The HEC became the most powerful government agency in Tasmania, creating entire new towns to build and manage its hydropower stations. Its up-to-date technological solutions included high-volume transmission lines to take cheap electricity to industry in the north and Hobart in the south, a first in Australia at that time. The power stations proved a model for later hydro schemes, including in the Snowy Mountains in New South Wales and Kiewa in Victoria.

The 'Hydro' became the largest employer in Tasmania, and by the late 1970s had 40 dams, including a dam on every major river in Tasmania except the Franklin. Energy-intensive industries had been created based on cheap hydropower, from canning factories to woodchip mills, paper manufacturing, aluminium and zinc smelting. At the same time, the loggers, best symbolised by the firm 'Gunns', were cutting down more and more forest for paper manufacture.

◀ Celebrated wilderness photographer Peter Dombrovskis took this photograph, *In the Great Ravine*, on the Franklin River in 1979.

In 1982, the pro-dam Tasmanian Liberal Party won a narrow victory and proceeded to authorise works to dam the Franklin River. Premier Robin Gray regarded the Franklin as 'nothing but a brown ditch; leech-ridden, unattractive to the majority of people'. In December, Bob Brown and thousands of others began a blockade that continued until March 1983. More than 1,400 people were arrested, including Brown himself and well-known British botanist and broadcaster David Bellamy. The Franklin issue spilled over into the 1983 federal election, where a Bob Hawke-led Labor Party defeated the Liberal/National Party coalition led by Malcolm Fraser. The Tasmanian Wilderness Society paid for the first full-colour newspaper advertisements ever to appear in a federal election campaign. Their 'no dams' slogan was accompanied by a striking Peter Dombrovskis photograph of the pristine river, with the telling question: 'Could you vote for a party that will destroy this?' The campaign captured the national imagination. Environmentalists had already been fighting canal developments, rainforest clearing and sand mining at many sites around Australia, but all could unite behind saving the Franklin.

On winning the federal election, incoming prime minister Bob Hawke announced that the dam would not proceed, claiming that the federal government had jurisdiction over the issue because of its international obligations under the World Heritage Property convention. Tasmanian Premier Gray and Queensland Premier Bjelke-Petersen challenged the issue in the High Court, which decided in a 4–3 vote in favour of the federal government's submission that it had the power to intervene in such matters. Previously, the state governments had always called the shots in land use decision-making, as land law in Australia is still state-based. Some states, most notably New South Wales, pressed ahead with new national parks, but Queensland persisted in canal development, bush clearing and sand mining.

In recent decades, Tasmania's economy has become more and more reliant on tourism, as manufacturing and forestry industries are in decline. Travellers from both the mainland and overseas are attracted by its pristine landscapes, from Cradle Mountain and the Freycinet Peninsula to the Franklin River and the south-west wilderness, as well as its picturesque convict ruins. The Franklin campaign brought the region's beauty to the attention of the world.

The victory gave enormous energy and national standing to Bob Brown, who later became the federal leader of the Australian Greens party, the most durable new political party to be formed in Australia in the last four decades. In the 1970s and 1980s, other notable environmental campaigns ushered in a new sense of appreciation of the Australian environment, from ending sand mining on Fraser Island to preventing further exploitation of the northern New South Wales rainforests. The Save the Franklin campaign stands out as the single most important turning point in Australians' appreciation of their natural environment.

Franklin dam protesters at the Liberal Party's federal election campaign opening at the Malvern Town Hall in Melbourne in 1983.

A colourful party welcomes the arrival of another boatload of supporters to the protest camp on the Franklin.

will destroy this?

Despite advice from his Attorney-General's Department that he has the power to intervene, Mr. Fraser has refused to prevent the flooding of the Franklin River.

Despite evidence that flooding the Franklin will be of little benefit to Tasmanians in providing power or creating jobs (the dam will add only 10% to Tasmania's electricity supply, fewer than 1,000 construction workers will be employed, and only 29 permanent jobs created), Mr. Fraser's Government has chosen to preserve peace in the Liberal Party rather than act to preserve an area of irreplaceable beauty.

If the Liberal Government is re-elected, this scene will be drowned; along with hundreds of other equally unique places.

Our concern is not politics, but the Franklin. Unfortunately, Mr. Fraser has made the Franklin a political issue.

And so we must ask you to vote for those parties committed to saving the Franklin.

Even though you may never have voted for them before and may never again.

We ask you, this once, to put Australia's heritage above party politics.

To vote, in the Senate, for the Australian Democrats.

And, in the House of Representatives,

Vote **1** ⚠ NO DAMS
MILO DUNPHY
AND PROTECT AUSTRALIA'S WORLD HERITAGE SITES.

VOTE FOR THE FRANKLIN
BECAUSE ONLY YOUR VOTE CAN SAVE IT.

National South-West Coalition
including Tasmanian Wilderness Society and Australian Conservation Foundation.

Authorised by Dr Robert Brown, Parliament House, Hobart.

◀ The first full-colour political advertisement ever published in an Australian newspaper made brilliant use of a Peter Dombrovskis photograph to bring home the message. Authorised by Dr Robert Brown (Bob), then a member of the Tasmanian parliament, it advocated a 'Vote for the Franklin', suggesting that Malcolm Fraser's Liberal government would not prevent a hydroelectric dam from flooding the pristine wilderness.

Stanley

Standing in the front garden of Highfield House, you see all of Stanley set out below you: the village, the harbour and 'The Nut', a massive, squarish volcanic plug, looming over the township. Few small towns in Australia have such a spectacular setting. The population of Stanley has rarely risen above 500, but this is part of the town's charm, as are its original buildings and streetscapes. Stanley is also the birthplace of Joseph Lyons (1879–1939), the only Tasmanian-born prime minister.

Highfield House ❶, built as a residence for the head of the Van Diemen's Land Company ❷ ❸ in 1832, became the centre of local society in Stanley. Formed in Britain in 1825, the company was granted a vast tract of land by Royal Charter and planned to breed fine wool. Settlers began arriving in 1826, and in 1842 the company had a township laid out by John Lee Archer, naming it Stanley after the Secretary of State for the Colonies.

Stanley quickly developed as the major port ❹ for northern Tasmania, especially because of its proximity to Melbourne. By the 1870s, it had butter, cheese and bacon factories, and sent fat cattle and sheep to Launceston and the West Coast mines, and potatoes to the mainland. The *Australian Handbook* of 1903 included a substantial entry on Stanley, demonstrating its importance at the time.

Joseph Aloysius Lyons was one of eight children born to an Irish couple in the small but thriving township of Stanley in 1879. His father, with little business acumen, lost all his money speculating on the 1887 Melbourne Cup, so at age nine Joe was sent to nearby Ulverstone to work as a farm labourer and apprentice printer. Two aunts from Stanley supported him when he returned there, age 12, to attend school. He became a qualified teacher in 1901, working at nearby schools. He stood for and won the state seat of Wilmot for Labor in 1909, advocating the breaking up of large country estates, free medical treatment for children and equal pay for women teachers. He went on to be premier of Tasmania (1923–1928) and then switched to federal parliament. Resigning from the Labor Party in 1931, he led the new United Australia Party to victory and served as prime minister until his death in 1939. The tiny cottage ❺ in Stanley where he was born is open to the public.

Shipping remained the primary link between Stanley, the rest of Tasmania, including Launceston with a weekly steamer, and Hobart, until the rail from Launceston reached the township in 1922. Two years earlier Stanley had lost the headquarters of the municipality to Smithton, 14 kilometres south-west, and the Van Diemen's Land Company moved its headquarters there as well. But Stanley's geographical location ensured the town's survival. In 1939, the Commonwealth government acquired 'The Nut' ❻ for postal and telegraphic services, with its own cable station, a key link in the cable from Tasmania to Melbourne.

◄ Despite resigning from the Australian Labor Party in the midst of the Great Depression, and leading the conservative United Australia Party to victory in the 1931 federal election, Joseph Lyons remained proud of his modest origins in Stanley. Here he is, as prime minister in 1935, outside the worker's cottage he was born in.

▲ William Purser painted Highfield House and its immediate setting in 1835, complete with horse and carriage, and a small protestant chapel in the background. The kangaroos and the gum trees were there to remind viewers that, while a house of that design might be found in England, the landscape was quintessentially Australian.

▼ The beach, township and 'The Nut', photographed from Highfield House in 2012.

Stanley managed to maintain a population of around 800 through the 1950s, with fishing, dairying, timber-getting, potatoes and turnips still underpinning the local economy. Its population fell in the 1960s and 1970s, and the closure of the railway in 1988 looked like a fatal blow. As in many other parts of Tasmania, tourists, attracted to both the nineteenth-century architecture ⑦ ⑧ ⑨ ⑩ and the natural beauty of the island, came to the rescue.

Today, Stanley depends for most of its income on tourism, augmented by a small fishing fleet. Its spectacular setting draws mainlanders on their road tour of Tasmania, whether they have brought their own car on the Melbourne to Devonport ferry or flown from the mainland and rented a car. Many of its historic buildings have been converted to accommodation, including an old bakery ⑪ and some of its late nineteenth- and early twentieth-century cottages are also available for rent. It is still a little off the beaten track, so a morning walk up 'The Nut' is not only invigorating, you may also have the track to yourself, sharing only with a wide variety of coastal bird life.

Explore the history

VICTORIA AUSTRALIA

Victoria

Bonegilla Migrant Camp

There's a man's job for you

'Un-Australian', a phrase that gained popularity in the 1990s, was used by *The Sydney Morning Herald* to describe a riot at Bonegilla in July 1961. Being housed in a former army camp, with too many meals of mutton and rabbit, made for an unhappy experience for many postwar migrants in the 1950s and 1960s. One Sunday in 1952, 600 men threw their plates of inedible spaghetti onto the ground in front of the camp director's hut, but tempers were calmed when Italian cooks were employed. Children, on the other hand, loved their first tastes of pineapple and watermelon, enjoyed the plentiful supplies of bread and jam, and ate Milo from the tin with a spoon. Eminent Australians who spent time at Bonegilla include scientist and author Dr Karl Kruszelnicki, engineer and businessman Sir Arvi Parbo, philosopher Raimond Gaita and soccer broadcaster Les Murray.

Most visitors to Bonegilla, the largest migrant camp in the nation's history, have a personal connection, either having arrived as a refugee or migrant or having relatives who started their Australian life at this camp. Attacks on multicultural Australia in the 1980s saw a renewed interest in Bonegilla both from former residents and their offspring. Reunions were held in 1987 and 1997 before the site became a museum open to the public in 2005. By then, both federal and state heritage agencies had listed the site, even though most of it had already been demolished by the army; the army was at least persuaded to keep Block 19 as a historic place. Because more than 320,000 migrants came through the camp between 1947 and 1971, many Australians have a connection and are keen to visit. This has been made easier since it was formally opened as a public heritage site.

To get to the Bonegilla camp, you come by car or bus. Depending on which direction you arrive from, you either pass the entry to the current Latchford Barracks, still in use by the army, or, from the Albury end, you drive through a sea of new suburbs and new shopping centres. As soon as you are on site, you get a sense of what it was like to arrive as a migrant during Australia's postwar migration boom.

If you were among the first migrants to come to Bonegilla, you saw a vast army outpost, with 24 army huts. All were pretty basic: roofing iron, weatherboard sides, wooden floors and no heating or cooling other than what the climate of northern Victoria had on offer. It could be bloody cold in Wodonga, under a tin roof, in winter. You may well have arrived at Station Pier in Melbourne by ship from Europe and then travelled by train to Wodonga. Over half of all displaced persons entering Australia between 1947 and 1953 came through Bonegilla, 170,000 in all. Many had endured great hardship, so their first real introduction to Australia, while very basic in terms of facilities, might still have been an improvement on the conditions they

◀ Images promoting the virtues of Australia to British and other European migrants often featured a strong, sunburnt male, thriving in a land of plenty. This Commonwealth government poster from 1947 indicated that both agricultural and industrial employment was there for the taking.

▶ This contemporary sculpture at the Bonegilla migrant camp uses roofing iron and rusted iron figures to capture something of the landscape of the camp as it may have appeared to newly arrived migrants.

▲ Volleyball at Bonegilla in 1950, with overflow tents for accommodation.

◀ Women and children settle into their quarters at Bonegilla in 1949.

had left in Europe. Some had lost family members on battlefields, in bombed cities and in concentration camps.

In the camp, women and children were normally separated from the men, as the army huts did not lend themselves to offering accommodation for married couples or larger family units. This changed in the early 1950s, when they were made more habitable and reconfigured to house families. Lured to Australia by posters and other propaganda that offered sunny skies, delightful beaches, sophisticated cities and jobs aplenty, an isolated army camp did not live up to some migrants' expectations of a new life. The comfort of their stay partly depended on how crowded the camp was, as occupancy levels could be as high as 4,500 or as low as 1,200. When full, the camp was a hive of activity, the downside being it could be very noisy and disconcerting for some, particularly those who were homesick.

Unlike at quarantine stations, of which Australia had a number, residents of Bonegilla were free to come and go. In the late 1940s and early 1950s, most stayed for four to five weeks, not least because they received instruction in English and learnt about 'Australian ways'. There were up to 1,000 trips a week to Albury on buses supplied by local proprietors. Wodonga traders lobbied the bus companies to drop people off at Wodonga instead. One hundred and twenty children from the camp got to travel to Benalla in 1954 to see Queen Elizabeth, the first visit by a reigning monarch to Australia.

Some new arrivals detested the camp, and there were minor riots, but nothing on the scale of protests in civilian prisons of that era. In 1952, there was a riot led by some Italians, upset that they hadn't been given work placements promised by the government and unhappy with the conditions in the camp. Improvements were demanded and more attention was then paid to the food served to particular ethnic groups. Sport became

▼ Many came to Bonegilla as refugees, but others came as migrants. Australia, in this government poster, offers sun and nutrients for all.

your family will flourish in AUSTRALIA

YOU CAN GO TO

AUSTRALIA FOR ONLY £10

youngsters under 19 travel FREE

ENQUIRE HERE NOW

a major focus, especially to channel the energies of younger males. The Bonegilla soccer team won the local competition in 1954.

By the mid-1950s, most newcomers were only staying a few weeks. The migrant groups who were most dissatisfied with the camp were the British and the Dutch, who had anticipated better living conditions. The issues of greatest concern for all, both refugees and voluntary migrants, were housing and jobs. Australia had an acute housing shortage after the Second World War, with wartime restrictions on building new houses continuing for some years. Overcrowding in expensive rental accommodation was endemic, especially in the larger cities. Adult males at Bonegilla, whether single or married, hoped for a job offer, but Australia rarely recognised their trade or professional qualifications, so many had to settle for jobs as labourers in the first instance. Some ended up working on the great public works projects of the 1950s, the Snowy Mountains and Kiewa Valley hydroelectric schemes. In 1961, another minor riot took place, involving German, Yugoslavian and Italian migrants, understandably frustrated with having nothing to do, at a time when a minor recession made it harder to find employment.

By the 1960s, the population of Bonegilla had fallen, with fewer migrants coming to Australia. Having originally vacated the site, the army began to reclaim accommodation huts and eating facilities, not least to house regular soldiers and conscripted youth training for the Vietnam War. Surplus residential huts were taken over for men working at the army's nearby Bandiana base.

While Bonegilla was the largest migrant camp in Australia, other large camps were to be found in all the capital cities and in major regional centres, including Newcastle and Wollongong. As the children of the postwar refugees and migrants reached adulthood, pressure mounted for more recognition of both their journey and the contribution they had made to Australian society. Substantial migration museums have been established in a number of centres; the first, in Adelaide, opened in 1986 during the state's sesquicentenary. The most prominent is the Immigration Museum in Melbourne, housed in a Customs House built by the colonial Victorian government and then ceded to the new national government after federation. Bonegilla remains the one camp where you can get a real sense of living conditions and the immediacy of the newcomers' exposure to the Australian bush.

WELCOME to BONEGILLA

Programme

I

1. RUSSIAN CHURCH CHOIR conductur FATHER GODJAEW.
2. SOPRANO - SOLO   Miss VISNIAUSKAS LECCIE.
3. POLONAISE - CHOPIN }
4. LA CAMPANELLA - LIST } Piano - Solo Mr TESZLERI ZOLTAN
5. BARITONE - SOLO   Mr BERGERS HARIJIS
6. HUNGARIAN DANSE   Miss LIPOWA OLGA.
7. UKRAINIAN CHOIR   conductur Mr STROOK.

II

8. ESTHONIAN }
   LATVIAN   } National Songs Miss HUIK BENITA
                                 Miss SAVITZKIS TIJA.
9. SAXOPHONE - SOLO   Mr PAAP CHARLIE.
10. IMMITATION   Mr OSKA ZYGFRYD
11. ACCORDEON - SOLO   Mr BURZEW
12. JOUGOSLAW NATIONAL SONG Mr SPASSIC
13. UKRAINIAN DANCE - CHILDREN
14. TENOR - SOLO (Hungar. Nat. Song) Mr KROYHERR VIKTOR
15. GYPSY - DANCE   Miss LIPOWA OLGA

Melbourne's Monuments

JOHN BATMAN

BORN AT PARRAMATTA N.S.W. 1800

DIED AT MELBOURNE 6TH MAY 1839

HE ENTERED PORT PHILLIP HEADS

29TH MAY 1835

AS LEADER OF AN EXPEDITION WHICH

HE HAD ORGANIZED IN LAUNCESTON V.D.L.

TO FORM A SETTLEMENT AND FOUNDED ONE

ON THE SITE OF MELBOURNE THEN UNOCCUPIED

THIS MONUMENT WAS

ERECTED

BY PUBLIC SUBSCRIPTION IN

— VICTORIA —

1881.

Memorials and monuments can tell us a great deal about our history, from their design and inscriptions to their placement in the landscape. Over 90 per cent of all memorials in Australia commemorate one or more wars, but many of our cities and country towns also have memorials to their 'colonial founders'. The appropriateness of celebrating 'founders' is now being questioned, especially if the inscription 'first settled in' is followed by a late eighteenth- or early nineteenth-century date.

War memorials can have commanding settings, including the Australian War Memorial, with its direct line of sight to both the old and new parliament houses, the Shrine of Remembrance overlooking St Kilda Road in Melbourne and the War Memorial in Sydney's Hyde Park. Sometimes the memorials are explicitly political, as in the case of the memorial to the Queensland Labor Premier T.J. Ryan, an advocate of Irish nationalism, whose statue, erected four years after his premature death in 1921, was sited deliberately so his back is turned on the protestant Queen Victoria, in Queens Park in Brisbane.

Two of our most historically intriguing memorials are just 500 metres apart near the centre of Melbourne. Melburnians, as residents of our wealthiest city in the nineteenth century, were keen on celebrating their history and their achievements. The memorial erected in 1881 to John Batman, abutting the Queen Victoria Market, announced in gold leaf that in May 1835 he had set out from Launceston, on behalf of the Van Diemen's Land Company, to 'form a settlement and founded one on the site of Melbourne, then unoccupied'.

Batman's treaties with Kulin Elders have been the subject of intense debate ever since. This was the most notable formal attempt by Europeans of some kind of arrangement with the Indigenous inhabitants, rather than just taking land by force or deception, but it was undoubtedly exploitative. In 2017, some people advocated the removal of a statue of James Cook in Sydney's Hyde Park, part of a debate about whether it is still justifiable to celebrate Australia Day on 26 January. In 1992, a small brass plaque was added to the Batman statue, and then amended in 2004 with stronger language, declaring that:

The City of Melbourne acknowledges that the historical events and perceptions referred to by this memorial are inaccurate. An apology is made to Indigenous people and to the traditional owners of this land for the wrong beliefs of the past and the personal upset caused.

This is one of the few occasions in Australia where civic authorities have faced the reality that the land our cities are built on once belonged to Australia's

◄ The John Batman memorial includes the inscription 'on the site of Melbourne, then unoccupied'. The small brass plate, with the apology, can be seen on the horizontal section just under that inscription.

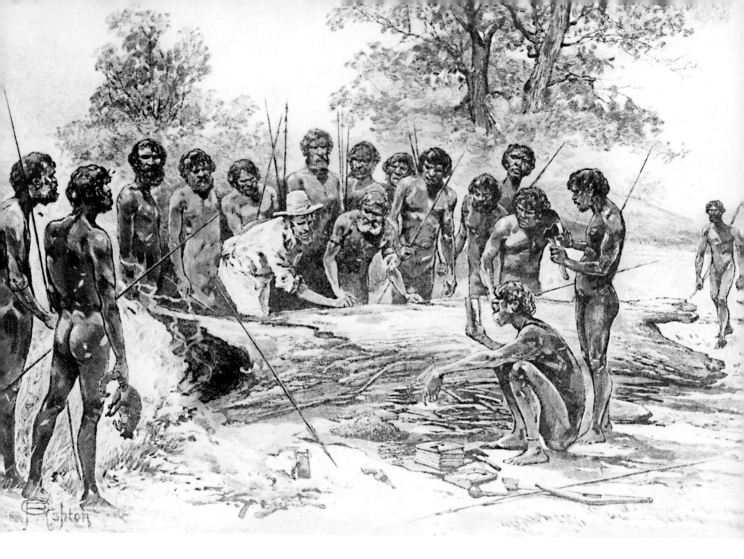

▲ British-born black-and-white illustrator George Rossi Ashton worked for a number of Australian magazines in the 1880s, when he produced *John Batman's Famous Treaty with the Blacks, Merri Creek, Northcote.*

Indigenous people. It is pleasing that the Melbourne City Council has not removed the memorial, nor changed its original inscription, but instead has chosen to acknowledge the context in which it was erected, and to reaffirm that the site of Melbourne was indeed occupied at the time of Batman's arrival. During his stint in Tasmania, Batman operated effectively as a bounty hunter, capturing and killing Tasmanian Aborigines for reward. He died at age 38 from syphilis.

Just up the road from the Batman memorial is the Eight Hour Day Memorial. James Galloway, a stonemason, convinced employers and employees to instigate the 8-hour day in February 1856. Two months later, stonemasons and other members of the building trades stopped work and marched to Parliament House, demanding implementation of the 8-hour working day. During this protest, the men waved banners with the intertwined 888.

In 1890, the Victorian parliament granted the pioneers of the Eight Hour Day movement a site in Spring Street for a celebratory monument. The pedestal and granite column, unveiled in 1903, had three figure '8s', topped with a sphere entitled 'Rest, Labor and Recreation'. In 1924, the monument was moved to the corner of Victoria and Russell streets, just up the road from the Queen Victoria Market, and opposite the Trades Hall. It remains a major gathering place for the annual May Day march and other labour movement marches.

◄ Percival Ball designed the Eight Hour Day Memorial, which stands on a Harcourt granite column, promoting eight hours' rest, eight hours' labour and eight hours' recreation.

Melbourne's Trams

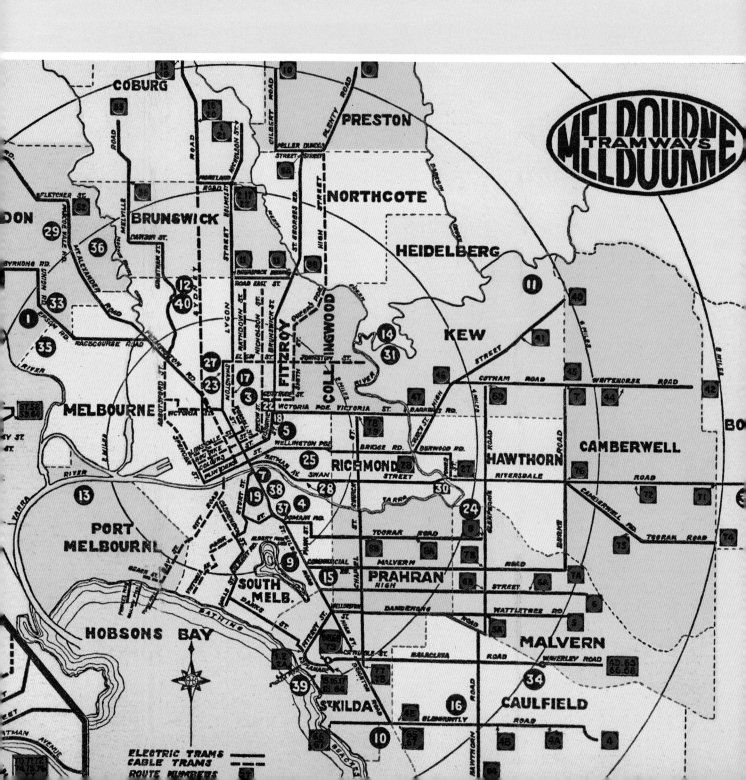

Today, Melbourne's trams are a long way from the picturesque cable cars of the 1880s, but they are still an inherent part of Melbourne life, for both the tourist and the commuter. Interstate drivers marvel as the ability of locals to make a compulsory hook turn in the city's centre, so that the trams are not held up. In the days of 6 o'clock closing, schoolgirls were told to be on the tram well before then because, after that, the trams would fill with inebriates falling out of the pubs and onto their transport home. After a long battle with trade unions, Melbourne got rid of all its tram conductors by 1998. Today, the system is easy to use and free in the immediate city area, while a myki card lets you explore the world's most extensive tramway system at a reasonable cost.

Trams are the visual centrepiece of Melbourne's grand city streets, from Collins and Swanston streets, to St Kilda Road and Victoria Parade. Even in some of the city's narrower shopping strips, most notably Chapel Street, Prahran, and Glenferrie Road, Hawthorn, trams are centre stage. Melburnians take their trams for granted, but for many visitors it is the first time that they have seen a vast tramway system in operation. Few people realise that Melbourne now has the largest tramway system in the world, as measured by track length, though not by numbers of passengers—that distinction is held by St Petersburg. Unlike other Australian capitals, Melbourne luxuriated in wide streets, so the tramways often got their own reservation, separate from horse-drawn traffic and later the car and the truck.

Growing up in a new 1950s subdivision on a former racecourse at Aspendale on Port Phillip Bay, we travelled into the city by train. We were well beyond the reach of the tramway system. Trams were a novelty to be savoured when we went to town, or visited relatives in closer-in suburbs. Melbourne's trams continued to operate when all other cities in Australia abandoned their networks. Its magnificent tramway terminuses are subject to heritage orders and have been well preserved. Modern trams have been introduced, better able to cope with disabled passengers, children and the elderly.

Well over 100 cities abandoned their tramway systems from the 1930s to the 1950s. The roads, which municipal or metropolitan authorities usually owned, could easily be reclaimed; tramlines could be simply covered over with bitumen. This happened throughout Canada, the United States, New Zealand, the United Kingdom, Ireland and Australia, with the notable exception of Melbourne's substantial network and Toronto's much smaller one. A mere handful of lines were kept in other cities, including in Glenelg in Adelaide, San Francisco's picturesque cable trams and New Orleans' Canal Street line.

◄ Melbourne's tramway system in the mid-1930s, with a few remaining cable tramlines still to be converted to electrical traction. Most Melburnians at that time lived within two kilometres of a train or tramline.

▲ A lithograph of Collins Street in 1889, with many tram passengers facing the elements. Melbourne's wide and elegant streets could still be very crowded long before the car and the truck came to dominance.

In Sydney, the tramway system, once bigger than Melbourne's, was removed and replaced with buses, as happened in London and all other large cities in the United Kingdom and the United States, along with most of Britain's former colonies. History happened in all these cities by the removal, not the retaining, of a key form of public transport. Sydney imported British experts who advocated getting rid of trams and embracing British-made Leyland buses.

Oil and motoring interests combined to campaign against trams. T.G. Paterson, the chairman of the thinly disguised lobby group deceptively called the Australian Road Safety Council, told the Melbourne *Argus* in 1948 that 'Trams are illogical vehicles, since they are really railways using the road for a track … Because they are confined to the centre of the road they are "road hogs"'.

The Melbourne and Metropolitan Tramways Board (MMTB), an independent statutory authority, had a long history of strong leadership, cemented with the appointment in 1949 of Major-General Robert Risson, then the assistant manager of Brisbane City Council's tramway department. Hailing from Australia's only capital city with a metropolitan-wide government, Risson came from a tradition of independence from the state government. The Brisbane City Council not only owned the trams and the tracks, but it owned the power station on the Brisbane River that powered the trams. And tramway employees were on the council payroll.

The MMTB continued to enjoy healthy patronage, and even though car ownership was increasing rapidly, the trams were still vital—with the railways—for the majority of journeys to work, and to get customers to and from the shops, whether in the city centre or along the great suburban shopping strips that the tram made possible. Some arterial tram routes had their own rights of way, including St Kilda Road, Dandenong Road, Royal Parade and Victoria Parade. At peak hour, the trams would be quicker than cars.

Tram patronage fell in Melbourne in the 1950s, but not as precipitously as in the other capital cities, where line closures were in full swing. Adelaide (maximum route length: 129 kilometres) and Perth (maximum route length: 55 kilometres) both closed their tramways in 1958. Auckland and Christchurch had closed theirs a few years before and Wellington had already abandoned half of its network, as had Sydney. The coming of television in the late 1950s saw a decline in cinema attendance, but both rail and tram remained vital in getting people to and from football games and the cricket, as they do to this day—Melbourne still draws greater numbers to sporting events than any other city. While Sunday drives became the preserve of the car, trams drove much of the action in inner and middle ring suburbs, from the journey to work, to school and to shop.

Major-General Risson inaugurated a house journal for the MMTB in 1964, to which both union members and management could contribute. In May 1966, it ran an article praising the purchase of new rolling stock:

> Why does Melbourne retain its trams? Because trams are eminently suitable for Melbourne … They are more efficient than buses … and they are many times more efficient than private cars, which eat up road space and carry, on average, less than 1.5 persons per vehicle … There is a tendency by some people and some authorities to suggest [the] scrapping of trams, and replacing them with a huge bus fleet … but Melbourne is well suited to trams. Its broad layout and wide streets, especially in the city, give it a place well ahead of congested cities—with narrow twisting streets like Sydney and London.

▼ Trams, horse-drawn drays and hansom cabs shared Melbourne's gas-lit streets in 1900.

Risson had, as a sometime ally, the nation's strongest tramway union, which managed to resist 'one man' operation for longer than in any other city. In New South Wales, the tramway union was promptly bought off with offers of employment in the rapidly expanding bus networks in Sydney and Newcastle. Tram depots were readily converted to bus depots, with the notable exception of the Fort Macquarie terminus at Bennelong Point, which made way for the new Opera House.

Melbourne's trams have long had pride of place as one of the city's most distinctive features. Trams continue to feature in most photographic and tourist representations of Melbourne from advertising posters to visitor maps of the city centre. Photographs of the Shrine of Remembrance, St Kilda Road, St Paul's Cathedral, the Arts Centre and Federation Square are invariably taken with trams in the foreground—by professional photographers and tourists alike. The quirkiness of some parts of the system is delightfully celebrated in the 1986 movie *Malcolm*. Trams were and remain the nearest Melbourne has to Sydney's ferries, long a core ingredient in that city's marketing and self-image.

The tramway systems of Eastern Europe, most of which had to be at least partially rebuilt after the war, continued in the 1950s and 1960s, before car ownership became widespread. Since then, many systems have reduced their route length, but patronage remains substantial. Around the world, from Manchester and Los Angeles to Sydney and the Gold Coast, new tramway routes are in the pipeline, sometimes reusing redundant rail corridors. While Melbourne today is only around the 200th largest city in the world—a long way from its top 20 listing in 1900—it can now lay claim to the largest tramway system on the planet, and what a civilising influence that is.

Old Melbourne Gaol

Melbourne Gaol, a grim and foreboding bluestone structure, served as the final home to more than 130 inmates in the era of capital punishment. Much of the gaol is now appropriated by an adjacent university. Prisoners lived in harsh, crowded and unsanitary conditions, subject to the vagaries of Melbourne's climate. Ned Kelly, bushranger and modern-day cult hero to some, was hanged here for his crimes. In a society where justice rarely favoured the poor, there were individuals who were wrongly incarcerated —and even wrongly hanged.

When you are taken on 'the Old Melbourne Gaol experience', men and boys, and women and girls, are split into gender groups, and both are placed in remand cells. The City Watch House and remand cells were in operation from 1909 to 1994. Inside each cell—where prisoners were held before being charged, or simply to sober up if unduly drunk or disorderly—up to 20 inmates sat or tried to sleep on wooden benches. A toilet pedestal within the room, open for all to see, couldn't even be flushed within the room; a warder operated a flushing mechanism from the corridor. It is a grim reminder of just how unpleasant and confronting most of our prisons were, from the original British occupation until the 1980s or even later.

Australia's convict settlements all, by necessity, had prisons. As the population grew, these prisons became substantial brick or stone structures, to thwart escape attempts. This is one of the reasons why so many survive to this day, now protected in all states by heritage orders. Today tourists flock to Fremantle Prison, Norfolk Island and Port Arthur, among many penitentiary sites in Australia. Nineteenth-century gaols were normally near the centre of population, while contemporary gaols are built on the outskirts of cities and country towns. The Castlemaine Gaol, which operated from 1861 to 1990, retains a commanding bluestone presence, erected at a time when the monumental visibility of a gaol was seen as a deterrent. The new replacement gaol is less obvious, located well away from the town. Other historic gaols, most notably Pentridge in Melbourne, have been converted into fashionable apartments.

Work started on Melbourne Gaol in 1841, reflecting the latest ideas of gaol design, especially from the new model prison of Pentonville in London. Solitary cells were thought to reform prisoners. High windows meant that prisoners could not see out from their cells, and escape was almost impossible, with bluestone walls 600-milimetres thick. Straw mattresses, one blanket and a toilet bucket were provided. The 'panopticon' plan meant that just a handful of warders could observe hundreds of prisoners. Two thousand prisoners were housed at the gaol between 1854 and 1856, for murder, theft, assault, arson, drunkenness and burglary,

◄ Old Melbourne Gaol remains an eerie place, even without the prisoners. A tour group can be seen on the ground floor in this photograph by Matt Chan, taken in 2013.

▶ A lithograph of Melbourne's Supreme Court and Gaol, published by Stringer, Mason and Co. in the early 1850s.

▲ This photograph of 'Ned Kelly, the Bushranger' was taken by Charles Nettleton the day before Kelly's execution.

▶ *Last Scene of the Kelly Drama: The Criminal on the Scaffold,* the work of Alfred May and Alfred Martin Ebsworth, 1880.

alongside people found to be of 'unsound mind'. Many prisoners who entered of sound mind, if eventually allowed to leave, took a long time to recover from the ordeal—and some never did.

Until the building of a female prison in Melbourne in 1864, women and children were placed in cell blocks, notionally separated from the men. Women were usually gaoled for vagrancy, which often meant they were homeless, or working as prostitutes.

More people were hanged at Melbourne Gaol than any other gaol in Australia. Of the 133 hangings between 1842 and 1924, four were of women. The first hangings were outside the gaol wall, making them a public spectacle. More than half of all hangings took place before 1865, including of a number of Aboriginal people, where the circumstances of their alleged crimes were often disputed, especially if they claimed to be defending themselves from attack.

The gold rushes had turned the colony of Victoria into one of the richest places on earth. Gold abounded but so did the temptation to rob banks, hold up coaches carrying gold or push a miner down his shaft to take over a lucrative lease. Such murders—popular in novels of the era—were hard to prove. Nonetheless, convictions for robbery, murder, rape and arson proceeded aplenty.

At 10am on 11 November 1880, the 25-year-old bushranger Ned Kelly was hanged at Melbourne Gaol, having been found guilty of the murder of Constable Lonigan in a dramatic shoot out at Stringybark Creek in central Victoria. Kelly was already a household name, because of audacious robberies and his ability to evade capture. No other hanging in Australia has ever seen so much publicity at the time or so much notoriety since. Scores of historians, novelists, filmmakers and painters have all tried to capture, if not capitalise on, the Kelly legend.

In 1842, John Kelly was transported from Ireland to Van Diemen's Land for stealing pigs. Ned Kelly was brought up by his mother Ellen, who on John's death had five daughters and three sons to look after. Growing up in a poor rural family, all the boys received gaol sentences for horse stealing and similar thefts. In 1878, Mrs Kelly was charged with aiding the attempted murder of a policeman and sentenced to three years' gaol, while Ned and his brother Dan had rewards posted for them. Four policemen set out to capture the two brothers, who promptly shot three of them. In the next few weeks, the two brothers and another gang member robbed banks at Euroa and Jerilderie. The gang was finally cornered by police at Glenrowan, and as the *Australian Dictionary of Biography* explains it:

Ned was protected by a cylindrical headpiece, breast and back plates and apron weighing about 90 lbs (41 kg). Little sleep and much consumption of alcohol affected their judgement and, although the armour limited their movements and use of firearms, it gave them a false sense of invulnerability. Under Superintendent Hare, the police surrounded the hotel and shooting began ... About 5 a.m. Ned returned, still clad in armour, looking huge and grotesque in the early mist. He was brought down by bullet wounds in the legs.

A reporter for *The West Australian* newspaper wrote a detailed account of the morning of Kelly's hanging:

About 9 o'clock crowds began to assemble in the gaol, and at 10 o'clock there could not have been less than 5,000 present, composed of a heterogeneous mob of men, women, and children, mainly of the lowest class. Those provided with tickets of admission to the execution presented themselves shortly before 10 o'clock ... The governor of the gaol then directed the executioner to do his duty. Upjohn came forward and placed the noose of the rope pendant from a strong beam overhead round the neck of the condemned man, who looked calmly at the priest in front of him, without paying any apparent attention to anything else going on around him. Dr. Barker instructed the executioner how to adjust the noose, and this having been done by placing the knot close under the left ear of the condemned man, while the cap was drawn closely over his head, covering his entire face, but leaving his heavy beard exposed. The executioner then stepped off the drop, and immediately the signal was given and the prisoner launched into eternity. The body fell about eight feet, and was brought up with a terrible jerk, Kelly being a large and heavy man. Death must have been instantaneous, as beyond a slight lifting of the shoulders and spasmodic quiver of the lower limbs no motion was visible after the drop fell.

Most visitors to what is now called the 'Old Melbourne Gaol' know of Kelly and his hanging. There is another hanging in Melbourne Gaol that deserves to be better known, but many people only learn about it if they visit the gaol. It is the case of Colin Ross, executed in 1922 for the murder of a 12-year-old girl, after the first conviction in Australia based on hair samples. The Melbourne *Herald* demonised Ross. Capitalising on public outrage, and relishing the increased sales, the paper offered a huge reward for the conviction of the killer, who had raped and then strangled the girl. Ross reaffirmed his innocence at the scaffold, in measured language. His family pursued the issue for decades, as did a number of journalists.

In 1998, the hair samples were reviewed, using modern techniques, and found not to be from Ross. Ten years later, he was posthumously pardoned by the Governor of Victoria, 86 years after his execution. By then, capital punishment had been abolished throughout Australia.

◄ Newspapers love to rehash past evil deeds, so 30 years after the murder of Alma Tirtschke that saw Colin Ross executed at the Old Melbourne Gaol he is denounced in Perth's *Mirror* as a 'brutal child slayer'.

Western Australia

Albany

Albany, the first permanent European settlement in Western Australia, began life as an outpost for the New South Wales government in 1826, fearing continuing French interest in the west. In the nineteenth century, its deep sea port made it the first and last stop for large steamers going to and from Britain, as well as for whalers. The smell of boiling blubber pervaded the town. Remarkably, the whaling station survived until 1978, the last to close in the English-speaking world. King George Sound, on whose shores Albany is located, was the last glimpse of home for departing soldiers heading off to conflict and an unknown fate in 1914. The National Anzac Centre, high above Albany, provides a spectacular view of the Sound and pays tribute to troops shipped off to the Great War from there.

lbany, on the southern coast of Western Australia, is situated on King George Sound, home to one of Australia's greatest sea ports in Princess Royal Harbour. While Dutch navigators recorded the southern coast in 1627, a British navigator, George Vancouver, claimed 'New Holland' for Britain in 1791, naming King George Sound after the then monarch. He reported on Aboriginal fish traps ① and noted a healthy population of seals and whales. British, French and American whalers took on supplies and repairs at Albany for the first half of the nineteenth century, but in the latter half of the century demand for whale products tapered off markedly, especially as kerosene and later coal gas replaced whale oil as fuel for lighting. Whalers went out from Albany longer than anywhere else in the English-speaking world, finally ceasing operations in 1978. Not only had they almost run out of sperm whales to kill, but the federal government, conscious of the United Nation's call for a moratorium on whaling in 1972, was preparing a *Whale Protection Act*, passed in 1980. The whaling station is now Whale World ②, where you can visit an intact processing factory.

The site now occupied by Albany began as a military outpost of New South Wales, partly out of concern that the French, following on from the charting of the coastline and the harbour by Nicolas Baudin in 1803, continued to take a close interest in this part of New Holland. In late 1826, Major Lockyer was sent by the New South Wales government with a small party of troops and convicts on the brig *Amity* ③ to establish the first permanent European settlement in the west and to confirm Vancouver's claim of the entire Australian continent for the imperial government in Britain. By 1831, the settlement was under the control of the newly established Swan River Colony, 300 kilometres to its north. The new settlers, resenting control by British governors based in Sydney, promptly requested that the Albany convicts and military garrison ④ be sent back there. The township grew relatively slowly in the following decades, gradually adding churches, schools

◁ A watercolour of King George Sound, painted in the early 1860s.

▲ This panoramic view of King George Sound, photographed by Darren Hughes in 2008, shows the landscape of the sound, where a well-located golf course revels in its coastal setting.

and municipal and government buildings, along with warehousing associated with the port.

By the 1880s, Albany had established itself as Western Australia's pre-eminent port ⑤, the first and last Australian port for all large ocean-going mail steamers, taking on coal and provisions before embarking on their long voyage. British, French and American ships were a regular sight in the port. Albany also served as the main port for the Western Australian goldfields, bringing a new source of revenue with the 1893 discoveries in and about Kalgoorlie.

The township revelled in a temperate climate, always important when marketing itself, both to the other side of the continent (whose inhabitants were called 'tother siders') and to the British colonies in Asia. *The Albany Guide*, published in 1890, pointed out that, if British families wanted to seek relief from the heat of India, Ceylon or the Straits Settlements, they should catch a steamer to Albany, a 'health resort'. Government and private schools catered to local children and some from the 'hot' inland districts boarded in the town.

The Colonial Office in London authorised the construction of a number of coastal forts around Australia, from Albany to Thursday Island, with colonial governments paying for construction and the British government supplying the armaments. By 1893, the Albany Fort ⑥ boasted six-inch guns that had a range of over eight kilometres.

Arriving by steamer, you saw a Court House ⑦, a Customs House ⑧, a Town Hall ⑨, the Police Offices and the Government Resident's abode ⑩, along with a Post and Telegraph Office ⑪, overlooked by the Princess Royal Fortress. Albany prided itself on its location behind the starting point of the Overland Telegraph

Line, putting it in 'communication with the civilized portions of the globe'. Albany also hoped to be the start of the intercolonial railway that would one day cross Australia. These hopes were soon dashed, with the route chosen for the 'Trans-Australian Railway' running from Sydney to Perth finally opening in 1917.

Albany lost its position as the main port in the west in the 1890s. As historian Don Garden explains, a 'band of parochial politicians' insisted that Fremantle become the colony's main port, even though that town required massive government funding for dredging, breakwaters and wharves to create a navigable harbour. Mail steamers, which had been calling at Albany since 1852, changed their Western Australian destination to Fremantle in 1898. Nonetheless, because of its deep harbour, Albany remained a key naval port, replenishing the 'Great White Fleet' of the United States navy in 1908. The port again came to national attention at the start of the Great War, when the first convoys of Australian and New Zealand troops, some accompanied by their horses, assembled in King George Sound.

The port town prospered from its rich agricultural hinterland ⑫, especially of wool and wheat. Wool mills ⑬ opened in 1925 and survived until early this century. Originally exported in bags, wheat and other grains are now shipped by bulk, along with wood chips. Bulk handling conveyors dominate the landward side of the port.

Tourism has been a mainstay for Albany's economy, although until recent decades most holiday-makers have come from within the state. Because of the distance from Perth, the city still gets very few international visitors. The Great Southern Railway from Perth opened in 1889, but passenger services ceased in 1978, so today you either have to fly on a propeller aircraft, catch a bus or drive.

◀ A souvenir postcard of welcome, produced to mark the visit of the United States fleet to Australia in 1908. Empire loyalty remains, with the American and British flags getting equal billing.

W. Fell photographed the first Australian troopships leaving Albany in 1914. Later killed, his negative was printed by Harold Cazneaux in the 1920s.

Most visitors drive, admiring both the coastal scenery and nearby vineyards. Albany finally got an international standard five-star hotel in 1991 at Middleton Beach, the dream of local entrepreneur Paul Terry. It was the fifth 'Esplanade Hotel' on the site, the first dating from 1898. Its predecessors had either burnt down or been demolished. Terry's hotel also housed an 'extravaganza gallery', displaying his $30 million-dollar collection of classic cars and artworks. As a novel touch, all items were for sale. Terry died in a helicopter crash in Honolulu in 1993 and the hotel changed hands, only to be demolished in 2007 by investors who then didn't replace it. A 13,000-square-metre hole has been there ever since, with the state government, out of embarrassment in a marginal electorate, buying the site for $7 million in 2014. No other site in Australia has had so many hotels on it, not even on the Gold Coast, where demolition is a way of life.

The National Anzac Centre **14** opened in Albany on 1 November 2014, exactly 100 years since 41,000 Australian and New Zealand troops headed off for the Great War. Located near to the Princess Royal Fortress, it offers a commanding view of King George Sound. The centre draws on the resources of the Western Australian Museum and the Australian War Memorial to offer visitors a rich portrait of the Anzac forces **15**.

Explore the history

1. **MENANG FISH TRAPS**
Oyster Harbour

2. **HISTORIC WHALING STATION**
Whaling Station Rd,
Frenchman Bay

3. **BRIG AMITY**
Residency Rd

4. **ALBANY CONVICT GAOL AND MUSEUM**
267 Stirling Tce

5. **PRINCESS ROYAL HARBOUR**

6. **PRINCESS ROYAL FORTRESS MILITARY MUSEUM**
Forts Rd

7. **COURT HOUSE**
184 Stirling Tce

8. **CUSTOMS HOUSE**
33 Stirling Tce

9. **TOWN HALL**
217 York St

10. **MUSEUM OF THE GREAT SOUTHERN (FORMER GOVERNOR'S RESIDENCY)**
Residency Rd

11. **POST AND TELEGRAPH OFFICE**
33 Stirling Tce

12. **OLD FARM, STRAWBERRY HILL**
174 Middleton Rd

13. **REMAINS OF WOOLLEN MILLS**
11–13 Mill St

14. **NATIONAL ANZAC CENTRE**
67 Forts Rd

15. **AVENUE OF HONOUR**
Apex Dr

New Norcia

The Benedictine monks who set out from Spain to establish a mission at Moore River, a four-day walk from Fremantle, had little sense of what awaited them. There, they founded New Norcia, which would grow to become a functioning township and self-supporting mission, where both Aboriginal and European children were educated—with very different futures in mind. The monastic community has persisted through time. Today, the town remains a place of spiritual retreat, catering to school and university groups. Tourists marvel at the nineteenth-century Spanish-style buildings, and most observe that the monastery still runs a large wheat farm. The museum offers a collection of post-Renaissance artworks dating from the sixteenth century, and provides an insight into the well-documented history of the town. You can explore the Abbey church, and visitors are often seen in conversation with monks going about their daily duties. In the heat of summer, a beer on the balcony of the hotel is popular with both locals and travellers.

Most visitors drive into Australia's only monastic town from Perth, 132 kilometres to the south. When I first visited, in 1984, Spanish buildings loomed, astonishingly, out of a flat landscape of wheat fields. There followed, on the left, a hotel, with locals enjoying a beer on its shady capacious verandas, a convent, two large boarding schools, with boys and girls spilling out into the playgrounds, a church, open to the public, and a monastery. The town had its own police station, service station, general store and a post office. I was visiting my uncle, who had just been appointed Prior Administrator of the Benedictine Community of New Norcia, which owned and operated the town. A Catholic convert from Anglicanism, he had graduated from the University of Queensland in the late 1950s and joined the Benedictine Order, undertaking his novitiate at Ampleforth Abbey near York in England and completing a doctorate in Theology at Fribourg University in Switzerland.

Due to the closure of monasteries by the Spanish government in 1835, two Spanish monks, Rosendo Salvado and José Serra, left Europe for Australia, arriving at Fremantle in January 1846. Setting out to establish a mission to the Aboriginal people, they walked with a dray for four days to reach a suitable site on the Moore River, among the Yued people of the Victoria Plains. They named the site New Norcia, after Norcia in Italy, the birthplace of St Benedict. Living by the Benedictine Rule, Salvado saw physical labour as a duty of existence. He left for Europe in 1849 to raise money for the monastery, returning in 1853. A school for Aboriginal boys, founded in 1848, was joined by St Joseph's Native School and Orphanage for Girls in 1861. Hundreds of Indigenous children were educated and trained by the

◄ The Abbey church, photographed in 1962 from inside the open gate of the Benedictine Monastery.

Spanish monks, including Mary Ellen Cuper, the first Indigenous person to be appointed to run a post office and telegraph station in Australia. As the telegraph was about to arrive in the region, the Superintendent of Telegraphs reported that Salvado had identified an Aboriginal woman 'who is perfectly familiar with the telegraph Code, and manipulation of the Key, and can read and write smartly'.

Many of the Spanish monks came from rural backgrounds, so they quickly adapted to growing wheat, and also to planting olives and grapes, staples of their homeland. At its peak, the community headed by Salvado consisted of approximately 250 people including 70 monks. Salvado also leased 960,000 acres over which he ran 22,000 sheep to support the mission. The second abbot, Torres, arrived in 1901. He went beyond the idea of the mission and embarked on creating a European-style monastic settlement, building two boarding schools to cater for the offspring of Catholic families in the region, some poor, some well off. He recruited Teresian Sisters from Spain to run St Joseph's Orphanage, Josephite Sisters from Sydney to run St Gertrude's school for girls (established in 1908) and Marist Brothers to run St Ildephonsus school for boys (established in 1913).

Some of the Aboriginal children had been forcibly removed from their parents by the Western Australian government, which, like the Queensland government, attempted to enforce a harsh regime of assimilation. The Aboriginal schools were closed in 1974, and from then on Indigenous boys and girls attended the two boarding schools. By the time my uncle arrived, in 1983, the remaining boarding schools were run down, and the Catholic teaching orders had departed. Allegations of child sexual abuse in earlier decades were coming to light. Better-off rural families now sent their children to boarding schools in Perth, while less well-off families relied on state schools in the region. The monastery had great difficulty recruiting good quality teachers to a rural area that was cold in winter, perishingly hot in summer and a good two hours' drive to the coast. By the end of 1991, the remaining small, co-educational boarding school

▲ Bishop Salvado, in working clothes—serge trousers, a blue denim shirt—and a prominent crucifix, in 1850. Salvado lived at New Norcia for 54 years. He died in Rome in 1900, and his remains were transported back to the monastic cemetery.

was no longer viable, so after some agonising within the monastic community, the school closed. The New Norcia Aboriginal Corporation, which dates back to the early 1990s, focuses on assisting members of the stolen generations and continuing dialogue between local Indigenous groups and the monastery.

In 1986, the monastery hit the national news, when 26 of its old master paintings were stolen, allegedly at the behest of a foreign buyer. Although some were cut out of their frames, they were all recovered. The monastery has over 50 historic buildings, listed on the Register of the National Estate, with an active plan for heritage conservation. Displays in the Museum and Art Gallery outline the Indigenous and European history of the monastery and the land. The strict Benedictine regime of prayers and contemplation continues, along with regular

▼ Aboriginal boys with a monk at New Norcia in 1910. All are barefoot, with hats to protect them from the hot summer sun.

choir practice. Visitors—Catholic and non-Catholic—are welcome at the guest house abutting the monastery, and women are allowed to use the monastic archives, a relaxation of the rules that didn't find favour with some of the older Spanish monks in the late 1980s. My uncle Selwyn who, reflecting a rather wicked sense of humour, had chosen as his monastic name Placid, was elected sixth abbot of New Norcia in 1997. He died on a visit to Ampleforth Abbey in 2008, and like previous abbots is buried in the New Norcia cemetery, between the two schools, now adapted for a variety of retreat, educational and musical purposes, including school camps.

When you walk up the hill behind the monastery, you survey a built landscape that has changed little since the hostel (later a licenced hotel) was opened in 1927. Then it was used by parents visiting children in the boarding schools. Now, you see wheat fields and plentiful olive trees. In the place of school children are a wide variety of visitors. Grey nomads and their vans, daytrippers from Perth, large school groups, relatives of former students and people from many different racial and religious backgrounds come to the monastery as a retreat and place of contemplation. The seventh abbot, John Herbert, currently oversees a small monastic community. The Abbey Church continues to be used by parishioners from the region, and New Norcia remains a functioning township. The monastery today, with its extensive archives, is a source for understanding changing attitudes to Indigenous Australians and learning more about agricultural practices as generations of Benedictine monks came to appreciate the Australian bush. A monastic daybook records the life of the monastery, an invaluable historical record of a place once very isolated, now linked to Perth by a fast road and to the world by the internet.

▲ Designed by Abbot Torres and built in 1908, the former St Gertrude's school for girls now provides accommodation for educational groups.

◄ The graves of the New Norcia cemetery, housing monks, members of teaching orders and other residents of the township, including both children and adults.

Islands

Cockatoo Island

Few of the world's large cities have an island where the past and the present are so closely juxtaposed. From a place of punishment, the island has evolved into a site for art events, maritime related workshops and a range of accommodation, from tents to heritage houses available for rent. Cockatoo became Australia's naval dockyard just before the outbreak of the First World War, building and repairing warships and submarines. When Singapore fell in 1942, it became the major shipbuilding and docking facility in the South West Pacific. While some of the structures from this period have been dismantled, visitors get a sense of the magnitude of the engineering work in the Turbine Shop and the Sutherland Dock. Wander through the Dog Leg Tunnel, built to move workers and material across the island and see nature's artwork in the layers of exposed sandstone.

At the junction of the Parramatta and Lane Cove rivers, Cockatoo Island marks the point where Sydney Harbour splits into these two rivers to the west. The only way to get to Cockatoo Island is by boat. Small craft and larger ferries have been delivering convicts, guards, reformatory girls, naval dockyard workers and now visitors to the island for well over 170 years.

Islands have long been favoured for imprisonment ➊ and often for military purposes as well. It is relatively easy to control who comes and who goes, usually with a single entry and exit point. With no water supply, and plenty of snakes, the first permanent occupants of Cockatoo Island were 60 prisoners from Norfolk Island. Housed in tents, with their overseers in hastily constructed huts, their first task was to build a wharf, barracks, guardhouse and kitchen. By 1842, there were 323 prisoners on the island, quarrying sandstone for the sea wall at Sydney Cove, today known as Circular Quay. As in most penal establishments, conditions were appalling. The prisoners were transferred to Darlinghurst in 1869.

In their place, came an industrial school for girls, including those under 16 who had been convicted of a crime. Wayward and orphaned boys were housed in the school training ship *Vernon*, moored just off the island. To make a new start, the establishment was renamed Biloela, after an Aboriginal word for Black Cockatoo. In 1871, the superintendent of the *Vernon* complained that 'semi-nude' girls came down to the ship 'blaspheming dreadfully', so he sent the boys to the lower deck 'to prevent them viewing such a contaminatory exhibition'. Three years later, a government inquiry found that the girls lived in awful conditions with cruel overseers, spending 12 hours a day in gloomy gaol cells formerly inhabited by convicts. In 1880, the girls were all withdrawn from the island, and sent to institutions in either Parramatta or Watsons Bay. The Biloela prison establishment remained in use until the early 1900s, when its inmates were transferred to Long Bay gaol, beyond Maroubra.

◄ Cockatoo Island in 1935 was a hive of industry, its two graving docks clearly visible along with the power station and its many workshops.

▲ Two workmen repair the propeller of HMAS *Australia* in 1930, one with pipe in mouth.

The first graving dock where ships were cleaned, the Fitzroy ❷ was built by convict labour between 1848 and 1857; it took so long because at that time activity counted for more than productivity. Sutherland ❸, the second and larger dock, was specifically built by the New South Wales government for the British navy between 1882 and 1889. Successive British admirals had lived at Admiralty House, opposite Circular Quay, and the government wanted Sydney to remain the continent's major port. In 1912, the new Commonwealth government having received the King's permission two years before to create a 'Royal Australian Navy', bought Cockatoo Island freehold from the New South Wales government for 96,500 pounds, paying another 750,000 pounds for the two wharves and all remaining buildings and equipment on the island.

The island has always been a commanding presence in the harbour, not least because of its tall sandstone outcrops and its role as a naval dockyard ❹, housing large cranes ❺ ❻ and assembly buildings ❼ ❽. During the Second World War, the dockyard employed up to 4,000 workers and operated day and night. The residents of the harbour-side suburbs of Woolwich and Balmain could hear the frenzied activity, though the island was off limits to all but authorised personnel.

My first visit, in 2005, was via a small motorboat from Woolwich, to assess the heritage significance of the remaining structures for the Sydney Harbour Federation Trust. The trust had been given responsibility to manage all former federal government property around Sydney Harbour, principally naval land and installations, such as the forts and defences at Clifton Gardens and Middle Head, and including gun emplacements and tunnels. With its myriad structures and artefacts, Cockatoo Island is the trust's most complex site. Before it was open to the public, the island had an eerie, abandoned feel, with rusting equipment, hundreds of loose roofing iron panels and rundown brick and sandstone buildings. Many of the more dangerous structures have been demolished, but the island remains a symbol of nineteenth-century incarceration and twentieth-century industry. By 2010, Sydney had lost most of its harbour-side industrial structures, including the Balmain and Pyrmont power stations and the huge gas plants at Waverton and Mortlake. Cockatoo Island is a fascinating survivor, with ample evidence of deprivation and enterprise across two centuries.

Charged with bringing new activity to the island, the trust now provides an array of overnight and longer accommodation, from the elegant houses **9** once occupied by senior medical and engineering staff to fully made-up tents and bedding along the foreshore, popular with backpackers and overseas visitors. The island has become a prime site from which to view New Year's Eve fireworks, along with rock music concerts and other organised activities, from art biennales to kayaking. It is readily accessible on the ferry from Circular Quay. While the island is no longer overrun with industrial structures, convicts or badly behaved girls and boys, you can still get a sense of isolation and wonder, from its tall cliffs, tunnels **10** **11**, convict-built silos **12** and two imposing graving docks. It is the best place in Sydney to be reminded of what the working harbour was like—when it was actually working.

Explore the history

1 CONVICT PRECINCT	**5** JIB CRANE Sutherland Dock	**9** BILOELA HOUSE
2 FITZROY DOCK	**6** SUBMARINE CRANE	**10** DOG LEG TUNNEL
3 SUTHERLAND DOCK	**7** TURBINE SHOP Industrial Precinct	**11** TUNNEL 1
4 MOULD LOFT Ship Design Precinct	**8** POWERHOUSE	**12** CONVICT SILOS

◀ By 2008, when this photograph was taken, many of the workshops had been demolished. Heritage-listed houses on the upper level remain and are now rented to the public. From Circular Quay, a regular ferry service docks at the wharf in the right foreground. The lawn area now provides tents for glampers, affording great views of Sydney and the New Year's Eve fireworks.

Norfolk Island

Prison, food bowl, hideaway: Norfolk has served many roles, with varied success. The worst convicts transported to Australia were confined to the island and treated without humanity. Revolt, rebellion and murder often followed. Some prisoners welcomed execution rather than continued incarceration in what has been described as 'hell in paradise'. Wild and isolated, even now supplies that arrive by boat need to be unloaded by whaleboats and launches. Descendants of the mutineers from the *Bounty* remain an important component of today's population and are fiercely independent. Explore the island's graveyard and see evidence of so many young lives abruptly ended. But there is one grave that suggests harsh punishment is not always a deterrent—its convict occupant died at 105! When driving around the island, remember to give way to livestock and to raise a finger (the Norfolk Wave) from the steering wheel in greeting.

Some places just reek of history and family mythology. Norfolk Island, created as a convict settlement in 1788, the same year as Sydney, is one such place. The first penal settlement, partly founded because Governor Phillip feared that Sydney might run out of food, itself had to be closed in 1814 because it couldn't feed its population. Thousands of petrel birds kept the convicts and their gaolers alive, but then the birds ran out. Reopened in 1825, the new penal settlement didn't purport to have agriculture as an aim; its purpose was to provide harsh punishment for secondary offenders. Maltreated convicts sometimes turned on and killed their gaolers.

Abandoned after the cessation of transportation in 1852, the second penal settlement left behind at Kingston ❶, along an excavated shoreline, a substantial gaol ❷ and commissariat store ❸, a mill ❹, a hospital ❺, saltworks ❻ and elegant Georgian dwellings ❼, including a commanding Government House (1829) ❽. Norfolk became a permanent home for 194 Pitcairn Islanders in 1856, courtesy of the intervention of Queen Victoria, as they could no longer survive on their tiny island. Led by George Hunn Nobbs, a reformed pirate who became an ordained minister in the Church of England, the population included offspring of the *Bounty* mutineers who had taken Tahitian wives, not least descendants of Fletcher Christian, the 25-year-old who led the mutiny against Captain Bligh, just ten years his senior. Public fascination with the mutiny on the *Bounty* story has resulted in five films since 1916. All the films appropriate the mutiny's history for their own purposes, including making the protagonists older. The first intrusion to the Pitcairners' new home was the establishment of a Melanesian mission ❾ in 1867; they had to learn to exist alongside the missionaries and their 'students' until the mission was relocated to the Solomon Islands in 1920.

◀ Kingston boasts a number of grand buildings, including the military barracks from the second settlement in the 1830s. Later used as the island's first Methodist church, the barracks provided a home for the Legislative Assembly. The building is sometimes occupied by protesters bemoaning the loss of self-government.

▲ This 1790 watercolour by George Raper included the explanation that 'the blue flag with the yellow cross is the signal hoisted when the landing is very good'. Norfolk Island still does not have an all-weather pier, so freight has to be offloaded onto smaller craft to get to shore.

According to recent archaeological evidence, Polynesians had lived on the island from around 1150 to 1450. By the time Captain Cook charted it in his 1774 voyage ❿, naming the island in honour of his patron's wife, the Duchess of Norfolk, it had been long uninhabited. Cook had high hopes for the Norfolk pines as a source of shipping masts, but the majestic trees proved too brittle for that purpose. The pines became a resource for shipping repairs, building and fuel for the early settlers—convicts, British military and Pitcairners. As a result, the volcanic landscape, measuring just eight by five kilometres, is now rather denuded, with steep hills and eroded gullies rolling down to jagged coastal cliffs, ending in rock shelves reaching out into the Pacific Ocean. Most of the island was carved up into hundreds of land parcels in the later nineteenth and early twentieth centuries and remains in private hands. Crisscrossed with a multitude of roads, Norfolk is hard to promote as an eco-destination, unlike Lord Howe, where the bulk of the island is national park and visitors walk and cycle, rather than drive. A small national park, created on Norfolk in 1985, reflects the earlier ecological richness of the island, but sea birds are best viewed from two small offshore islands ⓫.

For the first 150 years of settlement, contact with the outside world depended on shipping. American whaling ships from the Nantucket fleet would call in to take on provisions and make repairs, along with irregular visits from ships of the British Admiralty and supply ships. Norfolk finally got an airstrip in 1942, courtesy of the United States army and the New South Wales Department of Main Roads. Briefly manned by New Zealand troops, the strip proved too far from the Pacific War to have any strategic value. The islanders had long developed a strong sense of self-sufficiency, especially in agricultural produce. Norfolk is over 1,300 kilometres from the Australian mainland and 780 kilometres from Auckland, from where most supplies now originate.

Norfolk had its own small whaling industry in the nineteenth and early twentieth centuries. A more substantial whaling station **12** was established in 1955 but like Byron Bay closed in 1962, for the simple reason that they had run out of whales to kill. In the interwar years, the island exported bananas, lemon juice and passionfruit pulp, however neither of the island's small wharves was safe in bad weather; these fledgling industries foundered because of unpredictable shipping. After the war, the airport operated with a variety of carriers, enabling active tourist promotion of Norfolk as an exotic island with a dark convict history. Tourism boomed in the latter decades of the twentieth century as duty-free stores set up in what today appear to be tawdry buildings, some now abandoned in a straggling shopping strip.

◄ The surnames of the women and girls depicted in this 1857 photograph of Pitcairn Islanders included Young, Nobbs, Christian, Quintal and Evans. Their relatives can still be found on the island today.

◀ Cemetery Bay, Norfolk Island. The Norfolk pines provide an excellent windbreak for the golf course in the background.

▶ The cemetery, full of well-known island names, photographed in 1961. The cemetery is now better maintained and a popular site for tourists trying to comprehend Norfolk's complicated history.

The Commonwealth government granted Norfolk Island self-government, as an external territory, in 1979. With no income or company tax, the island lured some wealthy newcomers. Colleen McCullough, a neuroscientist who took up fiction writing, moved to the island after her novel *The Thorn Birds* became an international bestseller. She died in 2015 and is buried in the Emily Bay cemetery ⑬.

In a place that values and partly survives on celebrating its history, anniversary days loom large, from Foundation Day, marking British settlement, to Bounty Day, celebrating the arrival of the Pitcairners. Queen Elizabeth II visited in 1974 to mark the 200th anniversary of Cook charting the island. Heritage restoration received yet more funding in the lead up to the 1988 Bicentenary, with federal funds paying for a substantial upgrade to the four museums ⑭, all in convict-era structures. Norfolk's international reputation gained a great fillip in 2010 when the convict site at Kingston—dating from 1788, and including the wreck of the *Sirius* ⑮, which was lost just off Kingston in 1790 and whose artefacts were recovered in the 1980s— was inscribed on the World Heritage List, along with ten other Australian convict sites. These buildings sit in what the historian John Rickard has described as a 'well groomed park', including an immaculately kept nine-hole golf course.

With a population of 1,800 and up to 800 visitors a week, the island is home to proud descendants of the Pitcairners and more recently arrived residents. All are very conscious of their family and their island history. The local cemetary has graves from the two penal settlements, but it also has gravestones from the late 1850s bearing the family names that still populate the island—Adams, Buffett, Christian, Quintal and Nobbs. Two Anglican heritage churches remain in active use. Forty per cent of islanders are native-born, with the remaining population hailing from Australia and New Zealand. A vocal segment of the population is resentful that the Australian government removed their self-governing status in 2016, requiring islanders to pay income and company tax, but no GST. Today the island is jointly run by an elected local council and a Commonwealth government-appointed administrator, usually a retired politician, who resides in the graceful Government House. Islanders maintain a fraught relationship with the 'mainland', relying on it for social security payments and the upkeep of the World Heritage convict sites and the national park, but wishing to retain as much independence as possible.

Explore the history

1 KINGSTON AND ARTHURS VALE HISTORIC AREA

2 THE NEW GAOL
Kingston

3 COMMISSARIAT STORE
Quality Row, Kingston

4 CRANK MILL RUINS
Kingston

5 CIVIC HOSPITAL RUINS
Kingston

6 SALT HOUSE RUINS
Emily Bay

7 GEORGIAN BUILDINGS
Quality Row, Kingston

8 GOVERNMENT HOUSE
Quality Row, Kingston

9 ST BARNABAS CHAPEL AND MISSION SITE
Cnr Anson Bay and Headstone Rds

10 CAPTAIN COOK MONUMENT
via Duncombe Bay Rd

11 PHILLIP ISLAND AND NEPEAN ISLAND

12 PIER STORE MUSEUM
Pier St, Kingston

13 EMILY BAY CEMETERY
Emily Bay

14 NO 10 QUALITY ROW HOUSE MUSEUM
Quality Row, Kingston

15 HMS *SIRIUS* MUSEUM (FORMER PROTESTANT CHAPEL)
Bounty St, Kingston

Rottnest Island

Named 'rat's nest' by the Dutch explorer de Vlamingh in 1696, Rottnest Island has a dark history that is belied by its beautiful natural setting. The 'rats' are in fact quokkas and the island is a natural sanctuary with few predators to threaten their survival. It is also a birdwatcher's delight with coastal and migratory birds in abundance. The isolation from the mainland was once seen as ideal for an Indigenous prison, a reformatory for boys and internment camps for enemy aliens during both world wars. Longer-stay visitors are accommodated in a wide variety of heritage-protected structures, but the ever-present signage about the island's past means that it can no longer be glossed over or ignored.

I f visiting Rottnest Island in the 1960s or early 1970s, either by plane or boat, most travellers had the 'Island Playground' map, promising a 'carefree holiday'. The Surveyor-General's map showed happy figures fishing, swimming, hiking, sunbaking and learning to ride horses and play golf. All the family was catered for. Being an official government map, there were no advertisements. Holidaymakers were told they could stay in hostel or hotel accommodation, or in any of the more than 100 cottages, flats and bungalows available for rent or they could bring their own tent. Nowhere in the brochure was there any explanation of how all this holiday accommodation came to be; the only comment on the island's history was that a Dutch navigator had described it in December 1696 as 'delightful'. Willem de Vlamingh called it Rottnest, after the many 'rats'— the native quokka marsupial—that flourish on the island.

Many West Australians visiting Rottnest at that time would have known that it had been an Indigenous prison, an internment camp during the Great War and a military base in the Second World War, housing prisoners of war. None of this was mentioned in the official brochure, even though the same year maintenance workers on the island dug up skeletal remains of Indigenous occupants from the era of incarceration.

Visitors today are much better informed about the history of Rottnest, via brochures, websites and signage on the island. The Indigenous burial ground ❶ has now been fenced, and many aspects of the penal settlement explained in signage on structures now preserved under state government heritage acts. You can't take your own car to Rottnest Island, but visitors can cycle, walk or take the bus. The island remains a very popular holiday destination, both for daytrippers and longer stayers, and is now an official 'schoolies' site, so you are not able to escape all connection with the twenty-first century.

▼ Promoted as a bathing resort, this 1920s tourist brochure of the 'isle of girls nestling in an opal sea' features a demure, colour-coordinated young lady posing in the bathing costume of the era.

◄ Rottnest Island is today an idyllic setting for yachting, power boats and holiday makers.

For a Carefree Holiday

ROTTNEST ISLAND

WESTERN AUSTRALIA

INDIAN OCEAN

ARMSTRONG POINT

LI... ARM...

CHARLOTTE POINT

CITY OF YORK BAY

BARE HILL

CATHERINE BEACH

CRAYFISH ROCK

RICEY BEACH

STARK BAY

CELIA ROCKS

ABRAHAM POINT

... BEACH

WHITE HILL

MARJORIE BAY

ROCKY BAY

LADY EDELINE

HAYWARD CAPE

MABEL COVE

KING HEAD

CATHEDRAL ROCKS

EAGLE BAY

NARROW NECK

STRICKLAND BAY

GREEN IS.

MARY COVE

KITSON POINT

WILSON BAY

SOUTH POINT

CAPE VLAMING (WEST END)

FISH HOOK BAY

PREPARED BY THE MAPPING BRANCH, SURVEYOR GENERAL'S DIVISION, DEPARTMENT OF LANDS AND SURVEYS, PERTH WESTERN AUSTRALIA, IN COLLABORATION WITH THE ROTTNEST ISLAND BOARD
L.A. JONES   A.B. DAVIES
SUPERINTENDENT-MAPPING BRANCH   GOVERNMENT PRINTER
CROWN COPYRIGHT RESERVED...

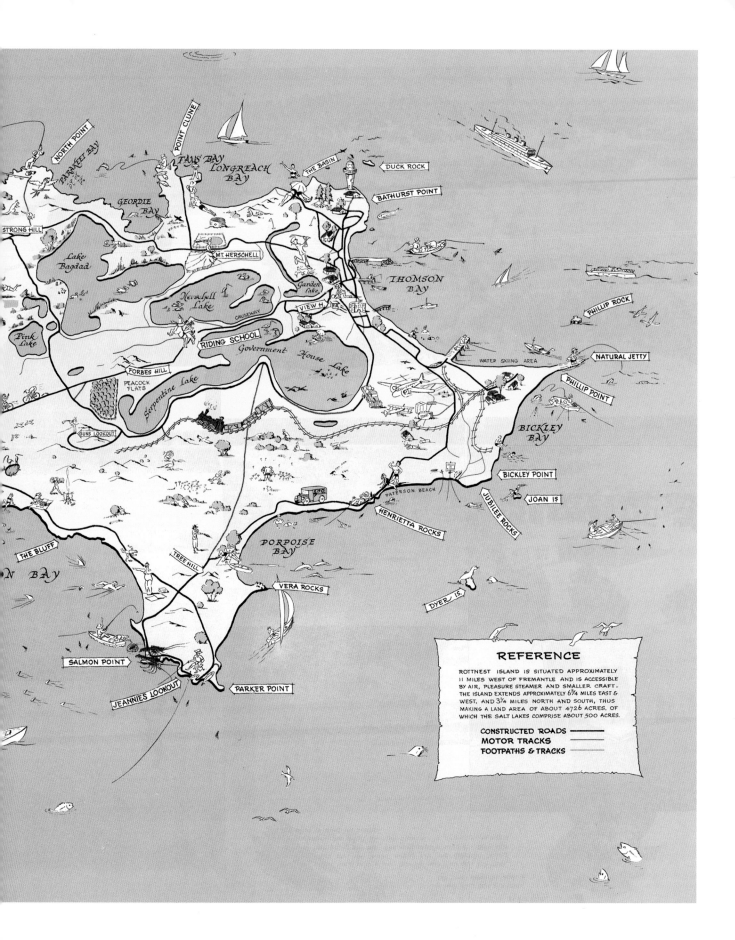

◀ As late as 1970, the Rottnest Island Board, a government body, promoted the island as a site for 'carefree' holidays, without any hint that it had long been a site of incarceration, especially for Indigenous people.

But it is hard to avoid confronting Rottnest's dark history, still so evident in many of the penal structures. Its military history is less confronting; the parade ground, overlooked by charming brick headquarters, looks more like a ceremonial private school building than a wartime relic.

When the colonial government of Western Australia decided, in 1838, to detain Indigenous offenders on the island, the Crown resumed control of all land, getting rid of a handful of European farmers. The Crown has owned all of Rottnest ever since, unlike a number of other inhabited islands, including Kangaroo, Lord Howe, Fraser, Stradbroke, Norfolk and the islands in the Whitsundays group. All these islands have Crown land, some are national parks but none is exclusively in Crown ownership. As the establishment on Rottnest grew, it contained an octagonal prison ❷, a chapel ❸, lighthouses ❹ ❺, salt works ❻ ❼, a flour mill ❽, military barracks ❾ and a sea wall ❿, giving the island a rather fortified feel, some of which it retains today. Most of the 3,700 people incarcerated there over six

decades were Indigenous, while some non-Indigenous prisoners were on the island as tradesmen. Over 300 prisoners died from mistreatment, disease or old age. Sentences varied from a few weeks to more than ten years, and five Indigenous men were executed on the island.

Charles Symmons, the 'Protector of Natives' in Western Australia, reported in 1843 on early construction on the island, including a stone building and vegetable garden.

All this has been effected within a period of fifteen months, by the labour of eight uncivilized and naturally most indolent natives, assisted solely by the superintendent, Mr Vincent, and a white prisoner, we are the more induced to regret that the natural unbiased inclinations of the aborigines of Western Australia should at present form such an inseparable barrier to their acquirement of any habits of industry or profitable activity.

▲ Aboriginal prisoners on Rottnest Island with their formally dressed guards, photographed by Archibald James Campbell in about 1890.

An inquiry into the Treatment of Aboriginal Native Prisoners in 1884 was less dismissive of the Indigenous occupants, demonstrating some concern for their welfare, criticising tiny cells and 'unsatisfactory sanitation'. Nonetheless, they recommended the prison continue, rather than transferring inmates to the mainland.

The great advantage of this Island Prison is that the natives can be worked without chains, and that they are allowed liberty on Sundays to roam at will about the Island … we have kept carefully before us the fact that it is not only our duty to deal with these poor unenlightened Aboriginals as merely the dispensers of punishment for offences committed, but we have also felt that we have a higher duty as well, viz., that during their imprisonment they shall be taught to respect the justice of our laws, returning to their native haunts benefited by those laws

The Indigenous inmates came from throughout the colony of Western Australia, and at the time of the Commission of Inquiry, many had come from Gascoyne and Murchison, where there had been 'bad seasons' and a 'scarcity of game', so some had taken to stealing supplies from local farmers. At Rottnest, the prisoners worked at quarrying, clearing land, salt works, vegetable gardening and building. Widgie Widgie Johnnie, who told the commission he was on the island 'for killing a native', said he had been brought to the prison by steamer from the north, with a 'chain round my neck all the way down. I was all right when I was in my own country'.

Closed in 1904, the gaol proved a ready-made site for an internment camp in 1914, housing Germans, Austro-Hungarians, Turks and Bulgarians, both prisoners of war and Australian citizens who were interned. In the Second World War, the Commonwealth government took up some of the land for a military base **11** and 200 Italian prisoners of war were housed there.

The Governor of Western Australia had a summer residence built for him on the island in 1864 **12**. This building fell into disrepair and became a hotel in 1953. Public tourism began in 1907 when the main prison building was converted into a tourist lodge. By the 1920s, the island had a hostel, general store and camping sites, and has been popular with the residents of Perth and other visitors ever since. Rottnest offers an intriguing array of historic structures, and visitors enjoy a range of accommodation options, all of which have their own history. Looking back at Perth from the island 100 years ago, you would have been hard-pressed to identify a single structure. But since Western Australia's mining boom, the metropolitan skyline is dotted with high-rise offices and apartments. Even when the boom goes bust, they will remain, sentinels to modern capitalism. Only 25 minutes by ferry from Fremantle, it is possible, on Rottnest, to escape the frenzy of city living, but the history of the island can no longer be easily ignored.

Explore the history

1. **WADJEMUP ABORIGINAL BURIAL GROUND**

2. **THE QUOD (OCTAGONAL PRISON)**
Kitson St

3. **ROTTNEST CHAPEL**
Thomson Bay settlement

4. **WADJEMUP LIGHTHOUSE**

5. **BATHURST LIGHTHOUSE**

6. **SALT STORE GALLERY AND EXHIBITION CENTRE**
Colebatch Ave

7. **SALT LAKES**
Geordie Bay Rd

8. **ROTTNEST MUSEUM (OLD MILL AND HAY STORE)**
Kitson St

9. **KINGSTOWN BARRACKS**
Kingstown Rd

10. **SEA WALL**
Thomson Bay

11. **OLIVER HILL BATTERY**
Defence Rd

12. **HOTEL ROTTNEST (FORMER GOVERNOR'S SUMMER RESIDENCE)**
Bedford Ave

References and further reading

There is a rich literature about Australia's events, people and places. This book draws on a number of key reference books, including: the ten-volume *Australians: A Historical Library* (1987); *Macquarie Atlas of Indigenous Australia* (2005) edited by B. Arthur and F. Morphy; *Historical Encyclopedia of Western Australia* (2009) edited by J. Gregory and J. Gothard; *The Wakefield Companion to South Australian History* (2001) edited by W. Prest; and *The Encyclopedia of Melbourne* (2005) edited by A. Brown-May and S. Swain. For Victoria, see the website victorianplaces.com.au, and for Queensland, see queenslandplaces.com.au, currently the only two states to have such websites. Biographies of many of the historical figures mentioned in this book are in the online version of the *Australian Dictionary of Biography*.

The mammoth *The Heritage of Australia: The Illustrated Register of the National Estate* (1981) remains the authoritative work of its era. All states now have regularly updated government heritage websites along with National Trust websites. Local histories are an invaluable source for events and places in particular localities, as are the strong local collections to be found in many municipal libraries. For readers wanting to see how a variety of authors have tackled history and place, see *Australian Historical Landscapes* (1984) edited by D.N. Jeans; *Journeys into History* (1990) edited by G. Davison; and *Symbols of Australia* (2010) edited by M. Harper and R. White. Readers wanting further information on people, places and events in this book are best advised to start with the National Library's Trove website—trove.nla.gov.au.

AUSTRALIAN CAPITAL TERRITORY **Making the Capital 'National'** Graeme Barrow, *Canberra's Embassies* (1978); Karen Fox, 'A City and Its People: Canberra in the ADB', Australian Dictionary of Biography website; Ken Inglis, 'Ceremonies in a Capital Landscape', in *Australia: The Daedalus Symposium* (1985) by S.R. Graubard; Peter Spearritt, 'Royal Progress: The Queen and Her Australian Subjects', in *Out of Empire: The British Dominion of Australia* (1993) edited by J. Arnold et al. **Old Parliament House** Ted Ling, *Government Records about the Australian Capital Territory* (2013).
NEW SOUTH WALES **Broken Hill** George Farwell, *Down Argent Street* (1948); Elizabeth Vines, *Broken Hill: A Guide to the Silver City* (2010). **Byron Bay** J. Davidson and P. Spearritt, *Holiday Business: Tourism in Australia since 1870* (2000); I.W. Morley, *Black Sands: A History of the Mineral Sand Mining Industry in Eastern Australia* (1981); Brunswick Valley Historical Society website; 'Cavanbah', Arakwal People of Byron Bay website. **The Cowra Breakout** Robert Virtue, 'A Japanese Perspective on the Cowra Breakout' ABC Central West NSW website, 4 August 2014; Chris Clark, *The Encyclopaedia of Australia's Battles* (2010); Harry Gordon, *Die Like the Carp!* (1978); Heritage Office & Department of Urban Affairs & Planning, *Regional Histories of New South Wales* (1996). **Myall Creek Massacre** Professor Lyndall Ryan et al, 'Colonial Frontier Massacres in Eastern Australia 1788–1872', The University of Newcastle's Centre for 21st Century Humanities website; New South Wales Legislative Assembly, Hansard, 8 June 2000; Alan Atkinson and Marion Aveling (eds), *Australians 1838* (1987); Henry Reynolds, *Frontier: Aborigines, Settlers and Land* (1996); C.D. Rowley, *The Destruction of Aboriginal Society*, vol.1 (1970); *Myall Creek Massacre and Memorial: Our Shared History* (2008). **Nutcote: Home of May Gibbs** R. Holden and J. Brummitt, *May Gibbs: More Than a Fairytale* (2011); 'Nutcote', Heritage Council of NSW website; *May Gibbs Interviewed by Hazel de Berg*, National Library of Australia, nla.cat-vn2147620; **The Sydney Opera House** *Sydney Opera House: World Heritage Nomination* (2006); 'Our Story', Sydney Opera House website.
NORTHERN TERRITORY **Darwin** Glenys Dimond, *Cyclone Tracy: An Unforgettable Christmas* (2004); Henry Frei, *Japan's Southward Advance and Australia* (1991); Douglas Lockwood, *Australia's Pearl Harbour Darwin 1942* (1966); Gary McKay, *Tracy: The Storm That Wiped out Darwin on Christmas Day 1974* (2001); Peter Read, *Returning to Nothing: The Meaning of Lost Places* (1996). **The Ghan** Basil Fuller, *The Ghan: The Story of the Alice Springs Railway* (2012); Simon Richmond, 'Journey through the Outback', *Geographical*, vol. 70, no. 3, 1998; C. Stevens, *Tin Mosques and Ghantowns: A History of Afghan Cameldrivers in Australia* (1989).
QUEENSLAND **Carnarvon Gorge** *Bennett Family Films*, 1957, John Oxley Library Collection; Jackie Huggins, Rita Huggins and Jane Jacobs, 'Kooramindanjie: Place and the Postcolonial', *History Workshop Journal*, no. 39, 1995; Danny O'Brien, *The Carnarvon Ranges* (1947); G. Walsh, *The Roof of Queensland* (1983). **Cooktown** Mark McKenna, 'On Grassy Hill: Gangaar (Cooktown), North Queensland', *From the Edge: Australia's Lost Histories* (2016); Glenville Pike, *Queen of the North: A Pictorial History of Cooktown and Cape York Peninsula* (1979); S.E. Stephens, *Introduction to Cooktown and District* (various editions). **Great Barrier Reef** James Bowen and Margarita Bowen, *The Great Barrier Reef: History, Science, Heritage* (2002); Clem Christesen, *Queensland Journey* (1938); Chloe Hooper, *The Tall Man: Death and Life on Palm Island* (2009); *The North Queensland Annual* (1968); G.K. Bolton, *Queensland's Great Barrier Reef* (1970). **Ipswich Railway Workshops** Queensland Historical Atlas website; Queensland Places website. **Warwick Railway Station** R. Archer et.al. (eds), *The Conscription Conflict and the Great War* (2016); F. Fitzhardinge, *William Morris Hughes*, vol. II (1979); D.J. Murphy, 'Thirteen Minutes of National Glory', *Queensland Heritage*, vol. 3, 1975.
SOUTH AUSTRALIA **Burra** Burra History Group website; B. Rowney, 'Kapunda-Burra', in *Australian Historical Landscapes* (1984) edited by D.N. Jeans; M. Walker and P. Marquis-Kyle, *The Illustrated Burra Charter* (2004). **Seppeltsfield Winery and Mausoleum** Seppeltsfield website; John Beeston, *A Concise History of Australian Wine* (2001).
TASMANIA **Port Arthur** David Young, *Making Crime Pay: The Evolution of Convict Tourism in Tasmania* (1996); Port Arthur Historic Site Management Authority website. **Save the Franklin** 'History of the Franklin River Campaign 1976–83', The Wilderness Society website; D. Hutton and L. Connors, *A History of the Australian Environment Movement* (1999); William Lines, *Patriots: Defending Australia's Natural Heritage* (2006); James McQueen, *The Franklin: Not Just a River* (1983). **Stanley** Marguerite Close, *Historic Stanley* (1988).
VICTORIA **Bonegilla Migrant Camp** Bruce Pennay, Various titles, including *Sharing Bonegilla Stories* (2012); Alexandra Dellios, *Histories of Controversy: Bonegilla Migrant Centre* (2017); Eric Richards, *Destination Australia: Migration to Australia Since 1901* (2008). **Melbourne's Monuments** Bain Attwood, *Possession: Batman's Treaty and the Matter of History* (2009); Monument Australia website; K.S. Inglis, *Sacred Places: War Memorials in the Australian Landscape* (2008). **Melbourne's Trams** *Light Rail Latest Figures* (2015), UITP website; Peter Spearritt, 'Why Melbourne Kept Its Trams', *12th Australasian Urban and Planning History Conference Proceedings* (2014). **Old Melbourne Gaol** National Trust Victoria's Old Melbourne Gaol website.
WESTERN AUSTRALIA **Albany** Douglas Sellick, *First Impressions: Albany 1791–1901 Travellers' Tales* (1997); Donald Garden, *Albany: A Panorama of the Sound from 1827* (1977); Peter Spearritt, *The Heritage Significance of Albany and Region: A Cultural Tourism Strategy Prepared for the Albany City Council* (1994); **New Norcia** New Norcia Studies, 1993–2015; David Hutchinson (ed.), *A Town Like No Other* (1995).
ISLANDS **Cockatoo Island** John Jeremy, *Cockatoo Island: Sydney's Historic Dockyard* (2005); The Sydney Harbour Federation Trust website; Godden Mackay Logan, *Cockatoo Island Dockyard Conservation Management Plan* (2007). **Norfolk Island** John Rickard, 'Norfolk Island', *Australian Historical Studies*, vol. 26, 1995; Peter Clarke, *Hell and Paradise: The Norfolk, Bounty, Pitcairn Saga* (1986). **Rottnest Island** R.J. Ferguson, *Rottnest Island: History and Architecture* (1986); *Rottnest Island: A Guide to Aboriginal History on Wadjemup* (1988).

List of illustrations

National Library of Australia images can be viewed in full by entering into your browser nla.gov.au/ followed by the image's identifier. For example, to see the first image below, go to nla.gov.au/nla.cat-vn1732969.

COVER front, top *Visitors at Heritage Site in Burra*, courtesy Heritage South Australia, Department of Environment, Water and Natural Resources, South Australia; **other images** repeated, refer to images in main text.
INTRODUCTION 2–3 John Goodchild, *Mount Gambier, the Lake District of South Australia*, 1930s, nla.cat-vn1732969; **4–5** repeated, refer to images in main text; **6** *Swan Hill: Centre of the Murray Valley … Where Past & Present Meet in the Sunshine*, Swan Hill, Victoria: Geographic Ephemera, nla.cat-vn4925319; **8** N. Murray, *Australia Welcomes You*, c.1969, nla.cat-vn5057665; **9** Ronald Clayton Skate, *ANA Serves 47 Towns and Cities*, 1950s, nla.cat-vn210445; **10** Caltex Oil Australia, *Motoring Tips for Holiday Trips*, 1950s, nla.cat-vn2695483, courtesy Caltex Australia.
AUSTRALIAN CAPITAL TERRITORY 12 James Northfield, *Canberra, Federal Capital & Garden City, Australia*, c.1930, nla.cat-vn2351243, © James Northfield Heritage Art Trust; **14** Sam Cooper, *Commonwealth Ave Bridge Looking Towards Parliament House at Night*, 2012; **16–17** R.C. Strangman, *Panoramic View from Mount Ainslie, War Memorial in Foreground, Canberra*, 1941, nla.cat-vn6154822; **19** 'This Week's Royal Tour Pictures Show … the Queen in Four Capitals', page 3 in *The Australian Women's Weekly*, 10 March 1954, trove.nla.gov.au/newspaper/page/4815207; **20** United States Information Service, *President Johnson Salutes the Crowd on Boarding the Aircraft and Mr Holt Is Seen Coming up the Steps, Canberra*, 1966, nla.cat-vn4406888; **22–23** Craig Mackenzie, *Aerial View of Capital Hill and Lake Burley Griffin, Canberra*, 2012; **24** Frank Hurley, *Parliament House with Reflections*, c.1938, nla.cat-vn90494; **26–27** King Billy, i.e. Jimmy Clements, *in Foreground of Parliament House*, 1927, nla.cat-vn3547995; **28–29** Col Ellis, *Panorama of Canberra Taken from Helicopter Platform*, 2013, nla.cat-vn6616667; **29 top** McCarron, Bird & Co., Melbourne, *Souvenir of Melbourne: Parliament House (Complete Design); The Treasury*, 1903, nla.cat-vn6448989; **30–31** Richard C. Strangman, *Old Parliament House, Canberra, with Sheep in Foreground*, 1940s, nla.cat-vn3773044; **32 top** *Dame Nellie Melba Singing God Save the King, Prime Minister S.M. Bruce and Mrs Bruce to Her Left*, 1927, nla.cat-vn3697250; **32 bottom** Australian Information Service, *Gough Whitlam Speaking on the Steps of Parliament House, Canberra*, 1975, nla.cat-vn2200376; **33** Greg Power, *Old Parliament House*, 2012.
NEW SOUTH WALES 34 F.G. Longstaff, *Delightful Views from the Carriage Windows: New South Wales Railways* (image digitally altered), c.1940, nla.cat-vn6616469; **36** Peter Myers, *View of Broken Hill CBD*, 2016, www.flickr.com/photos/myersphotography/30487034315, reproduced under CC BY 2.0: creativecommons.org/licenses/by/2.0/; **38** Fred Hardie, *Broken Hill Proprietary Mine, New South Wales*, c.1892, nla.cat-vn4557520; **39** Joyce Evans, *Barrier Social Democratic Club Inc., Broken Hill*, 1996, nla.cat-vn2307231; **40–41** Frank Hurley, *Aerial View, Broken Hill*, between 1910 and 1962, nla.cat-vn89754; **42** Robin Smith, *Moslem Mosque, Broken Hill*, 1977, nla.cat-vn4236273, courtesy Robin Smith; **43** Joyce Evans, *House of Israel, Former Synagogue, Broken Hill*, 1996, nla.cat-vn784658; **44 top** Stephen Fleay, *Pro Hart at Work in His Studio, Broken Hill*, c.1980, nla.cat-vn5983233; **44 bottom** Wolfgang Sievers, *Miners at North Broken Hill Mine, Broken Hill*, 1980, nla.cat-vn2496011; **46** BentR, *Byron Bay, Surfing at Sunset*, 2014, pixabay.com/en/byron-bay-beach-new-south-wales-2317741; **48** Carol Neuschul, *Byron Bay Hippies*, 2010, www.flickr.com/photos/pixculture/5254183710, reproduced under CC BY-SA 2.0: creativecommons.org/licenses/by-sa/2.0/; **49** Michael Terry, *Whale on a Jetty, Byron Bay*, 1960, nla.cat-vn6980383; **50–51** BigTo, *Lighthouse, Byron Bay*, 2010, commons.wikimedia.org/wiki/File:Byron_Bay_Leuchtturm.jpg,

reproduced under CC BY 3.0: creativecommons.org/licenses/by/3.0/deed.en; **52** Lee Pearce, *More Than 2000 People Demonstrated against Over-development in Byron Bay*, 2004, nla.cat-vn3547782; **54** 'War Prisoners Escape from Camp', *Sunday Telegraph*, 6 August 1944, nla.cat-vn786229; **56–57** *Blankets Thrown over the Barbed Wire in B Camp, by Escaping Prisoners*, 1944, Australian War Memorial, 073485; **58** *A Number of Knives and Other Improvised Weapons Found in and around B Compound of the Cowra Prisoner of War Camp Immediately after the Mass Escape*, 1944, Australian War Memorial, P02567.003; **59** Richard Gifford, *Japanese Gardens, Cowra*, 2005, www.flickr.com/photos/rgifford/158454632, reproduced under CC BY 2.0: creativecommons.org/licenses/by/2.0/; **60** Michael Terry, *Track Nearing Myall Creek, New South Wales*, 1971, nla.cat-vn6240406; **62** Samuel Thomas Gill, *The Avengers*, c.1860, nla.cat-vn458787; **63** 'Australian Aborigines Slaughtered by Convicts', in *The Chronicles of Crime, or The Newgate Calendar* by Camden Pelham, 1891, nla.cat-vn1697507; **64** Peter Spearritt, *Myall Creek Massacre Memorial*, 2016, courtesy Peter Spearritt; **66** Kim Woods Rabbidge, *Nutcote, at Kuraba Point, Overlooks Neutral Bay*, 2015, courtesy Kim Woods Rabbidge; **67** May Gibbs, *The Complete Adventures of Snugglepot and Cuddlepie*, 1946, nla.cat-vn2818021; **68** Harold Cazneaux, 'Nutcote', Home of C.M. Kelly (May Gibbs), Neutral Bay, New South Wales, c.1926, nla.cat-vn3121217, courtesy the Cazneaux Family; **69** May Gibbs, cover of *The Lone Hand*, January 1916, nla.cat-vn1211693; **70** Stephen Edward Perdriau, *Map of Part of the Water Frontage of the Port of Sydney*, 1908, nla.cat-vn7294652; **71** Robert James Wallace, *The Sydney Opera House and Sydney Harbour Bridge Illuminated by Night Lights*, 2007, nla.cat-vn3971272; **72–73** John Tanner, Australian News and Information Bureau, *Aerial View of Bennelong Point with Trams, Sydney*, 1958, nla.cat-vn4593083; **74** Ern McQuillan, *Aerial View of the Sydney Opera House Nearing Completion*, c.1967, nla.cat-vn3795824; **75** Jørn Utzon, *Architect's Model for the Geometry of the Sydney Opera House Shells*, 1961, nla.cat-vn530583, courtesy Jan Utzon.
NORTHERN TERRITORY 76 *Go by Train to Central Australia for Winter Holidays*, 1950s, nla.cat-vn5880357; **78** *Oil Storage Tanks Burning after Being Hit during the First Japanese Air Raid on Darwin during World War II, Darwin*, 1942, nla.cat-vn5126064; **80–81** Darren Clark, *View of the Esplanade Taken from Old Admiralty House, Darwin*, 2010, nla.cat-vn5177355, courtesy Darren Clark; **83 top** *USS Peary Burns Behind HMAS Katoomba, with HMAS Manunda on the Right, after a Japanese Air Raid, Darwin*, 1942, nla.cat-vn5126065; **83 bottom** Franck Gohier, *Darwin 1942*, 2014, nla.cat-vn6972976, courtesy Franck Gohier; **84** Bruce Howard, *Tracy—She Broke His Heart: The Morning after Cyclone Tracy Devastated Darwin, Casuarina Resident Lynn John Cox Returned from Holidays to His Wrecked Home*, 1974, nla.cat-vn3076160; **86** *The Ghan Locomotive, NSU-51, at Alice Springs Railway Station, Northern Territory*, 1954, nla.cat-vn4181735; **88–89** *The Ghan*, Railways—Ghan: Ephemera, nla.cat-vn2594535, courtesy Great Southern Rail; **90** *Adelaide to Darwin 2004, Inaugural Year, The Ghan*, Railways—Ghan: Ephemera, nla.cat-vn2594535, courtesy Great Southern Rail; **91 top** Frank Hurley, *An Afghani Man Loading a Heavily Laden Camel Train*, 1914, nla.cat-vn6097686; **91 bottom** John Tanner, Australian News and Information Bureau, *The Ghan Diesel Locomotive at Alice Springs, Northern Territory*, 1958, nla.cat-vn4590340.
QUEENSLAND 92 M. Anderson, *South Queensland Surfing Resorts: The Beaches Are Calling*, c.1935, nla.cat-vn6577642; **94** Peter Boer, *Carnarvon Gorge Art Gallery*, 2013, www.flickr.com/photos/minuseleven/15752753062, reproduced under CC BY 2.0: creativecommons.org/licenses/by/2.0/; **96–97** Will Brown, *Carnarvon Gorge, Boolinda Bluff*, 2016, www.flickr.com/photos/37428634@N04/28860209885, reproduced under CC BY 2.0: creativecommons.org/licenses/by/2.0/; **99 top left** *Aboriginal Rock Paintings at Carnarvon Gorge*, 1938, John Oxley Library, State Library Queensland, image number 6403-0002-0012; **99 top right** *Aboriginal Rock Painting*

Index

The publishing imprint of the
National Library of Australia

Title: Where History Happened: The Hidden Past of Australia's Towns and Places
Author: Peter Spearritt
ISBN: 9780642279262
Published by NLA Publishing
Canberra   ACT   2600

© National Library of Australia 2018
Text © Peter Spearritt

Books published by the National Library of Australia further the Library's objectives to produce publications that interpret the Library's collection and contribute to the vitality of Australian culture and history.

Commissioning Publisher: Susan Hall
Managing editor: Jo Karmel
Editor: Amelia Hartney
Designer: Susanne Geppert
Image coordinator: Jemma Posch
Production coordinator: Melissa Bush
Printed in China by The Australian Book Connection

The author would like to thank the editorial and production team at the NLA, listed above, who were a delight to work with. He would also like to thank Yvonne Byron for her suggestions, and his accommodation providers in Canberra, the Callanan, Foster and Young households.

Find out more about NLA Publishing at publishing.nla.gov.au.

A catalogue record for this book is available from the National Library of Australia